Armor of God
Prayers for Protection and Deliverance

Written and compiled by Dave Juliano

Armor of God

Copyright 2006 by David Juliano
ISBN978-0-9777223-2-7

Published 2006 by In the Shadows Publishing
Printed by CafePress.com in the United States of America

Armor of God

Thanks to Jamie, Jill, Leslie, Kristyn and John Zaffis

Dedicated to Christ Church and Fr. Paul

Armor of God

Table of Contents

Introduction

1. Hedge Prayers

2. Protection for a Household

3. Protection from Curses or Spells

4. Personal Protection

5. Spiritual Warfare

7. Prayers to Archangel Michael

8. Exorcism

9. Deliverance

Armor of God

Introduction

What is a prayer? Does it have any real power?
Words are more powerful than most of us realize.
Whenever we create a thought or put intentions
behind something we say, we are creating real
physical energy. When we say a prayer for
protection we are creating positive energy which
helps create a barrier against negative energy. The
simple answer is yes, there is true power in prayer.

Many prayers ask for assistance from God, Angels,
Saints and numerous other higher spirits. There
are many higher level spirits know as Ascended
Masters, Teachers, etc. depending on the culture.
They are all here to assist us throughout our lives.
Some are very specialized and others can be called
on whenever you are in need. They are real and
they will help, all you have to do is ask. Each
religion has their own way of asking for protection
from God and you'll be surprised to see how
closely they resemble each other even though the
name of God may be different. This book is a
collection of prayers that I have saved from various
sources over the years.

If you are going to use this book as a tool to help
others, remember to consider their belief system
and not force yours upon them. This is why I
have included prayers from a variety of religions in
this book.

7

Armor of God

I am a Christian. I was a baptized Catholic and confirmed Episcopal. I am not a follower of one set organized religion but I respect them all. As a student of history I have seen that many of the tenets that make up the world religions are universal. We are all tied in more closely that you know. Given my primary belief system, I use Christian based prayers, and this book includes a majority of these. I am Episcopal but I still use many Catholic prayers and ask the Saints for assistance which is something that is not really associated with the Episcopal Church. Even within religions there are divisions, but don't let this stop you from utilizing a prayer that has worked well for others.

Many of these prayers are called prayers of exorcism. Exorcism is not just a Catholic ritual. Almost all world religions have a form of exorcism. Exorcism is also misunderstood thanks to Hollywood and a handful of high profile cases. Exorcism simply means to clear or expel by or as if by incantation, command, or prayer. Did you know that if you were baptized by a Catholic priest you had an exorcism done to you during the ceremony? It's a part of the Catholic Ritual of Baptism. Exorcisms are used to clear out of habitually negative obsessions, remove any negativity from a location, removing the influence of other spirits upon us and driving out demonic entities.

1. Hedge Prayers

Hedge Prayers are very strong protection prayers. It creates a large and thick hedgerow made up of dense bushes and trees. Anything that is bad for you gets caught up in the branches of the hedges but light and positive thing pass through easily. The first time I did this I had my own doubts about it but I put my faith behind the prayer. I never mentioned that I did this to anyone. The next day a friend who is psychic came to my house and told me that he saw my hedge around my house and the outside of it was covered with debris caught up in the branches.

Hedge Prayer for Protection of Household

Trusting in the promise that whatever we ask the Father in Jesus' name He will do, I(we) now approach You Father with confidence in Our Lord's words and in Your infinite power and love for me(us) and for our household and family, and with the intercession of the Blessed Virgin Mary, Mother of God, the Blessed Apostles Peter and Paul, Blessed Archangel Michael, my(our) guardian angel(s) and the guardian angels of our household and family, with all the saints and angels of heaven, and Holy in the power of His blessed Name, as ask you Father to protect our household and its members and keep us from the harassment of the devil and his minions.

Father I(we) ask in desire to serve You and adore You and to live our lives for You that You build a hedge of protection around our household, like that which surrounded Job, and to help us to keep that hedge repaired and the gate locked so that the devil and his minions have no access or means to breach the hedge except by your expressed will.

Father, I(we) am(are) powerless against the spiritual forces of evil and recognize my(our) utter dependence on You and Your power. Look with mercy upon me(us) and upon our household and family. Do not look upon our sins, O Lord; rather, look at the sufferings of your Beloved Son and see the Victim who's bitter passion and death has reconciled us to You. By the victory of the cross, protect us from all evil and rebuke any evil spirits who wish to attack, influence, or breach Your hedge of protection in any way. Send them back to Hell and fortify Your Hedge for our protection by the blood of Your Son, Jesus. Send your Holy Angels to watch over us and protect us.

Father, all of these things I(we) ask in the most holy name of Jesus Christ, Your Son. Thank you, Father, for hearing my(our) prayer. I(we) love You,

I(we) worship You, I(we) thank You and I(we) trust in You. Amen.

Hedge Prayer for Protection of Others

Trusting in the promise that whatever we ask the Father in Jesus' name He will do, I now approach You Father with confidence in Our Lord's words and in Your infinite power and love for me and for ___*[person's name]*___, and with the intercession of the Blessed Virgin Mary, Mother of God, the Blessed Apostles Peter and Paul, Blessed Archangel Michael, my guardian angel and the guardian angels of ___*[person's name]*___, with all the saints and angels of heaven, and Holy in the power of His blessed Name, as ask you Father to protect ___*[person's name]*___ and keep him from the harassment of the devil and his minions.

Father I ask on behalf of ___*[person's name]*___ that You build a hedge of protection around him, like that which surrounded Job, and to help ___*[person's name]*___ to keep that hedge repaired and the gate locked so that the devil and his minions have no access or means to breach the hedge except by your expressed will.

Father, I know that we are powerless against the spiritual forces of evil and recognize our utter dependence on You and Your power. Look with mercy upon ___*[person's name]*___. Do not look upon his sins, O Lord; rather, look at the sufferings of your Beloved Son and see the Victim who's bitter passion and death has reconciled us to You. By the victory of the cross, protect ___*[person's name]*___ from all evil and rebuke any evil spirits who wish to attack, influence, or breach Your hedge of protection in any way. Send them back to Hell and fortify Your Hedge for his protection by the blood of Your Son, Jesus. Send your Holy Angels to watch over him and protect him.

Father, all of these things I ask in the most holy name of Jesus Christ, Your Son. Thank you, Father, for hearing my prayer. I love You, I worship You, I thank You and I trust in You. Amen.

Hedge Prayer for Protection of Self

Trusting in the promise that whatever we ask the Father in Jesus' name He will do, I now approach You Father with confidence in Our Lord's words and in Your infinite power and love for me, and with the intercession of the Blessed Virgin Mary, Mother of God, the Blessed Apostles Peter and Paul, Blessed Archangel Michael, my guardian angel, with all the saints and angels of heaven, and Holy in the power of His blessed Name, as ask you Father to protect me and keep me from the harassment of the devil and his minions.

Father I ask that You build a hedge of protection around me, like that which surrounded Job, and to help me to keep that hedge repaired and the gate locked so that the devil and his minions have no access or means to breach the hedge except by your expressed will.

Father, I know that I am powerless against the spiritual forces of evil and recognize my utter dependence on You and Your power. Look with mercy upon me. Do not look upon my sins, O Lord; rather, look at the sufferings of your Beloved Son and see the Victim who's bitter passion and death has reconciled us to You. By the victory of the cross, protect me from all evil and rebuke any evil spirits who wish to attack, influence, or breach Your hedge of protection in any way. Send them back to Hell and fortify Your Hedge for my protection by the blood of Your Son, Jesus. Send your Holy Angels to watch over me and protect me.

Father, all of these things I ask in the most holy name of Jesus Christ, Your Son. Thank you, Father, for hearing my prayer. I love You, I worship You, I thank You and I trust in You. Amen.

A Hedge around a Family

I claim a hedge of protection around myself, spouse and children (family) throughout this day and night. I ask you GOD, in the name of JESUS to dispatch angels to surround me, my spouse and my children and grandchildren today and to put them throughout my home, our cars, souls and bodies. I ask angels to protect my house from any intrusion and to protect me and my family from any harmful demonic or other physical or mental attacks. I ask this prayer in the name of JESUS. Amen.

2. **Protection for a Household**

These prayers are specifically meant to protect
Families. I've included generic Christian prayers as
well as a Pagan one.

Resisting Satan's Attack Against Our Household

In the name of the Lord Jesus Christ, strengthened
by the intercession of the Immaculate Virgin Mary,
Mother of God, of Blessed Michael the Archangel,
of the Blessed Apostles Peter and Paul, and all the
Saints and Angels of Heaven, and powerful in the
holy authority of His name, *and by my authority as
head of the household,* I(we) come before You
Heavenly Father to ask you to come against the
powers of darkness causing *(name whatever symptom)*.

Come against these powers, O Lord, because of the
power of my(our) union with the Lord Jesus Christ.

Armor of God

According to Your Word, O Lord, and through His precious blood I(we) resist the devil and his minions.

I(we) resist the devil and all of his workers by the Person and power of the Lord Jesus Christ. I(we) submit *(and submit this household)* to the Lordship and control of the Lord Jesus, and I(we) as you Father to bring the power of my(our) Lord's incarnation, His crucifixion, His resurrection, His ascension, His glorification, and His second coming directly to focus against all evil forces and all of the evil work against _____. *(By the authority of my position as head of the household),* I(we) claim my(our) union with the Lord Jesus Christ, and I(we) resist the devil; I(we) resist the devil and all his minions, and I(we) ask You heavenly Father to force these evil ones to flee from before the truth of God.

Further, O Lord, I(we) ask You to bind together the whole kingdom of the evil one and to bind them from working, and finally to command all evil forces and their kingdom to leave _____ and to go where the Lord Jesus Christ may sends them. Amen.

Armor of God

General Prayer

Visit this house,
we beg you, Lord,
and banish from it
the deadly power of the evil one.
May your holy angels dwell here
to keep us in peace,
and may your blessing
be always upon us.
We ask this through Christ our Lord.
Amen.

Rebuking Particular Spirits Affecting the Household

In the name of the Lord Jesus Christ, strengthened by the intercession of the Immaculate Virgin Mary, Mother of God, of Blessed Michael the Archangel, of the Blessed Apostles Peter and Paul, and all the Saints and Angels of Heaven, and powerful in the holy authority of His name, *and by my authority as head of this household,* I(we) ask of the heavenly Father to rebuke this spirit of _____ and to command it in the name of the Lord Jesus Christ to depart from *(me, family member)* and from this household, now, quietly, without harm to anyone. I(we) bring the power and the protection of the blood of our Lord Jesus Christ over this household, *(and over particular family member)*. Satan has no part in this household or with any member of my(our) family. This family and household is sealed with the saving blood of the Lord Jesus Christ.

Heavenly Father, forgive me(us) and my(our) family for not being all we should be in Your eyes. Let the cleansing, healing waters of our baptism wash over this me(us) and this household and cleanse me(us) and it from all unrighteousness.

Lord Jesus Christ, fill me(us) *(and a particular family member)* with Your *(attribute opposite to that of the spirit being rebuked)* to replace the *(attribute of the spirit being rebuked)* .

Lord Jesus, bring to bear all the guardian angels of this family, and all the angels of heaven, against the forces of evil that seek to cause trouble for me(us) and my(our) household.

Saint Michael, be our protection against the wickedness and snares of the devil. Blessed Virgin Mary, Mother of God, and our Mother, pray for us that we may not fall into the devil's temptations.

Thank You, Heavenly Father, for setting us free. We praise You, We bless You, We worship You. Thank You for the wisdom and light of the Holy Spirit.

Thank You for enabling me(us) *(and/or "me" as head of the household)* to be aggressive against the works of the enemy. Thank You for Your hope, that takes away discouragement; thank You for ongoing victory. *"...in all these things we are more than conquerors through Him who loved us"* (Romans 8:37). Amen.

Prayer For Salvation Of Children

Oh, Father...my Father in heaven. I come to You in the precious name of Your Son, JESUS. Today I submit myself to You and Your will for my life. I ask Father that you will forgive me for any unconfessed sin and mistakes in my life according to Your promise in 1 John 1:9. I want nothing in my life to hinder Your answering this prayer. Thank You, Father, for granting to me the privilege of interceding for someone else. How great and awesome You are!

Father, I come to You in behalf of _____.

He/she does not realize that they're in the middle

of a spiritual battle. I believe that the powers of darkness, satan's evil angels are having an influence in _____'s life. JESUS promised His followers' authority over Satan and his evil angels in Mark 16:17 and Matthew 12:29, Father. I want to claim that authority right now in the event that it is demons who are harassing him/her.

Now demons, forces of darkness, listen. In the mighty name of JESUS CHRIST I command you to take your hands off of _____ and get out of his/her life. I claim him/her for JESUS and plead the merits of His precious blood to cover_____ until they can claim it for himself/herself. In JESUS' mighty name I bind you and cast you where He wants you to go.

Father...Father, I ask that You will back up this authority with the power of Your HOLY SPIRIT and angels that excel in power and strength. I commit this child into Your hands according to Your promise of 2 Timothy 1:12, that You will take care of that which I commit to You until that day!

Also, Father, bind _____with cords of CHRIST's blood, hedge him/her in so that no evil can prevail in their life. And if there are people in _____'s life that satan or his demons are using to influence him/her the wrong way, I urge You to turn them away and make it so that they cannot stand each others presence.

Thank You, Father, that You have made all the resources of heaven available to those seeking to save the lost. Thank You for hearing and answering this prayer, because I ask it in the precious name of JESUS. Amen.
[This prayer may also be used for other family members and friends].

Prayer for Protection of the Home

Goddess of the hearth, beat strong and pure in the heart of my home.
Lord of the threshold, keep vigilant guard over the entrance to my home.
Spirits of the land, keep watch throughout the yard of my home.
God of the borders, stand ready to repulse all disorder from my home.

3. Protection from Curses or Spells

Curses and Spells can have real power over believers and non believers alike because of the thought and intent that went into the curse or spell. This can create a real force against you. By using prayer, you are affirming your belief that you can break the hold of any curse or spell.

Breaking Household Curses and Spells

In the name of the Lord Jesus Christ, strengthened by the intercession of the Blessed Virgin Mary, Mother of God, of Blessed Michael the Archangel, of the Blessed Apostles Peter and Paul, and all the Saints, and powerful in the holy authority of His Precious and Wondrous Name, We ask, O Lord God, that you break and dissolve any and all curses, hexes, spells, seals, satanic vows and pacts, spiritual bondings and soul ties with satanic forces, evil wishes, evil desires, hereditary seals, snares, traps, lies, obstacles, deceptions, diversions, spiritual influences, and every dysfunction and disease from any source whatsoever, that have been placed upon our family and household; [and particularly upon ___*[person's name]*___, whom we love very much.]

Father in Heaven, please rebuke these evil spirits and their effects and cast them away from this family [and particularly upon ___*[person's name]*___] so that we may continue to do Your Will and fulfill the mission you have for them to Your Greater Glory.

Thank you, Father, for hearing our prayer. We praise Your Holy Name and worship You and Love You. Thank You for the wisdom and light of Your Holy Spirit. Thank You for enabling us through Your Holy Spirit to be aggressive against the works of the enemy. Thank You for Your Hope, that takes away discouragement; thank You for ongoing victory. "...in all these things we are more than conquerors through Him who loved us" (Romans 837).

Father, We now place our enemies into your hands. Look with mercy upon them, and do not hold their sins against them. Anyone who has cursed our family and household, we now bless. Anyone who

has hurt us, we now forgive. For those who have persecuted us, we now pray
Our Father...
Hail Mary...
Glory Be...
O My Sweet Jesus, forgive us our sins and save us from the fires of Hell. Lead all souls to Heaven, and help especially those who are most in need of Thy Mercy.

Holy Michael the Archangel, defend us in battle. Be our protection against the wickedness and snares of the devil. May God rebuke him, we humbly pray; and do thou, O prince of the heavenly hosts, by the power of God, thrust into hell Satan and all the other evil spirits who prowl through the world seeking the ruin of souls.
Amen and Amen.

<u>A Binding Prayer</u>

I bind all curses that have been spoken against me. I bless those who curse me, and pray blessing's on those who despitefully use me. I bind all spoken judgments made against me and judgments I have made against others. I bind the power of negative words from others, and I bind and render useless all prayers not inspired by the HOLY SPIRIT; whether psychic, soul force, witchcraft or counterfeit tongues that have been prayed against me.

4. Personal Protection

The prayers in this section cover a variety of different religions.   Many of these prayers can be used every day and some are for more specific times. The prayers are for your own personal protection from harm, evil and danger.

Prayer for Filling of The Spirit

Lord Jesus Christ, I want to belong to You from now on. I want to be free from the dominion of darkness and the rule of Satan, and I want to enter into Your Kingdom and be part of Your people. I will turn away from all sin, and I will avoid everything that leads me to wrongdoing. I ask You to forgive all the sins I have committed. Come into my heart as my personal Savior and Lord. I offer my life to You, and I promise to obey You as my Lord and Master. I ask You to fill me with Your Holy Spirit. Amen.

Prayer For Protection

Heavenly Father, I come before you to ask for your protection against the powers of darkness, which comes to disrupt my life. You are my shield and my fortress, and my refuge when I am in distress. There is no one stronger than you Lord. I trust in you Lord. In the name of Jesus, I call out the angelic host for full protection of my mind, soul and body. Thank you Lord for watching over me. In the name of Jesus no weapons formed by Satan against me will prosper. Come Holy Spirit, and help me to put on the Armor of God, according to Ephesians 6:10. I put on the belt of truth because Jesus is the Truth, and the Truth set me free; I put on the breastplate of righteousness to protect my body and my heart as I walk in righteousness; I put on the shoes of peace as I walk in obedience to You Lord, and go wherever to Spirit takes me; I put on the shield of faith to protect me against the fiery attacks of the enemy; I put on the helmet of salvation to protect my mind and my salvation; I take hold of the sword of the Spirit which is the Word of God, to defend myself against Satan and demolish his strongholds. Thank you Lord for your full watchfulness and full protection. I give you

Lord all the praise, and honor, and glory forever. In Jesus name, I pray.

Prayer for Protection

The Light of God surrounds me;
The Love of God enfolds me;
The Power of God protects me;
The Presence of God watches over me;
Wherever I am, God is,
And all is well.

Armor of God

Prayer To Put On The Armor Of God

"put on God's armor so as to be able to resist the devil's tactics." I stand my ground "with truth buckled around my waist and integrity for a breastplate..." I carry the "shield of faith" to "put out the burning arrows of the evil one ..." I accept "salvation from God to be my helmet and receive the word of God from the Spirit to use as a sword" (Eph. 6:10, 11, 14, 16, 17 NAS)

Standing Guard While I Sleep

"Father God, please send your Holy Angels to stand guard over me today (tonight). I pray that they will minister to me and remind me of your healing power. Lord please keep me safe from the evil one and strengthen me against all temptations that may come my way. Thank You Lord, in the name of Jesus Christ, I pray, Amen."

Armor of God

Be My Shield

"Lord God, please surround me with favor as with a shield today. Lord, please strengthen Your wall of protection around me, keeping me safe from temptation of the flesh, tricks of the Adversary, and all harm. Lord, please fill my thoughts with Your thoughts and let my words be your words. You are my strength, my shield and my defense, O Lord. Thank You, Lord, in Jesus name I pray, Amen."

Guardian Angel Prayer

Angel of God, guardian dear, to whom God's love commits me here, ever this day be at my side, to light, to guard, to rule and guide. Amen.

The Full Armor of God

"Plead my cause, O Lord, with those who strive with me; fight against those who fight against me. Take hold of shield and buckler, and stand up for my help. Also draw out the spear and stop those who pursue me. Say to my soul, "I am your salvation." Let those be put to shame and brought to dishonor who seek after my life; let those be turned back and brought to confusion who plot my hurt. Let them be like chaff before the wind, and let the angel of the Lord chase them. Let their way be dark and slippery, and let the angel of the Lord pursue them. In Jesus Christ, Amen"

"Heavenly Father, I praise and worship you because you are God. I am honored to be your servant and I take my stand today against the devil and his schemes against me, my family and my ministry. Father, as I take up each piece of the armor, please secure it in place on me.
I take up the shield of faith and extend it over myself. It extinguishes all the fiery darts of the evil one.

Armor of God

I put on the helmet of salvation, which protects my mind from the enemy's attacks. I have the mind of Christ."

I put on the breastplate of righteousness, which covers my body with the righteousness of God. In Christ, every foothold of evil has been washed away and I am clothed in righteousness!

I gird my loins with the belt of truth. Your word, O God, is truth. Father, sanctify me according to your word and remind me through the Holy Spirit of the truth that destroys the lies of sin.

I shod my feet with the preparation of the Gospel of peace. I have peace with God through the blood of Jesus. I have favor with God and with man. I walk in my inheritance as an adopted son of God and have authority over evil in Jesus' name.

I will use the Sword of the Spirit by speaking the Word of God as it applies to whatever situation I may face today. Father, please remind me of your Word via the Holy Spirit.

I will continue throughout the day praying in the Spirit, and I believe that the Holy Spirit is interceding on my behalf according to my prayers.

Thank you, Father, for the whole armor of God. Please surround me with your hedge of protection as I move forward on the spiritual battlefield today. I praise and worship you now and forever, Amen."

<u>Prayer For Protection</u>

O Father, I am so thankful JESUS said we could call You, our Dad; it is so much easier talking with You. Father, Your Word says You are our refuge and strength [Psalm 46:1] and that You can do the impossible. _____ needs Your protection in a BIG way. Please watch over and keep him/her safe from the dangers, traps, and temptations, Satan's cohorts have intended for <u>him/her</u> today. Hedge _____ in, Father, with the merits of JESUS' shed blood.

JESUS prayed in John 17:11-20 for You not to take us out of this world, but to keep us from the evil in it, this is my prayer, too. Not to be taken out of it, but that You, by Your HOLY SPIRIT and angels that excel in strength and power, will give _____, as well as me, strength, courage, and protection to live in this world.

Thank You, Father, for hearing my prayer and answering it according to Your will. In JESUS' name, Amen.

Prayer for Protection

Beloved Angels of God,
Beloved Masters of Wisdom, Peace and Love,
Beloved Lady Masters of Heaven,
Beloved Elder Brother, Jesus the Christ,
Beloved mighty St. Germain,
Beloved Heavenly Father and Mother
Who are in heaven as on earth,
We come before You
Asking for your heavenly help In all things that we do.
We ask for your holy protection always
So that the work we are meant to do in this world
Will not be disrupted or delayed in any way,
But will proceed with
The greatest of ease, peace, and blessings.
We are grateful for all the Good
We have been able to do by Your Grace up until now.
And so we come asking for further protection

Armor of God

At all times and in all situations
So that we can continue to serve the Will of God.
We call for round-the-clock protection
Around our homes and the places that we work,
eat, and play.
We call for solid protection
Around our loved ones at all times as well,
That they can never be used as pawns or tools of
darkness
Which is only ignorance of God's Love.
Keep us always in the brightest Light.
Keep us immune to the negative pulls
Of the planets, people, or spirits.
Keep us happy and seeing the Truth in every
situation,
And free of judgments against our brethren.
And keep us always alert to potential dangers
Coming from any source whatsoever,
Whether seen or unseen,
Known or unknown,
Embodied or disembodied.
And may we always have an avenue
Of escape from danger or mishap
Whenever necessary.
Let us truly be instruments of the Divine,
Seeing clearly what would be
The best course of action to take, if any,
In every situation that we see.
Speak words of wisdom
And counsel into our listening ears

Armor of God

And see to it that we are always surrounded
By angels of light, protection, wisdom and love.
Let us truly reflect
The Presence of God
On earth as it is in Heaven.
See to it that our lives are filled with
Laughter, joy, and love always.
And may we be empowered to bring
These same blessings into the lives of
All those we contact.
Let healings occur in our presence
And miracles, too.
Lord Michael before, Lord Michael behind
Lord Michael to the right, Lord Michael to the left
Lord Michael above, Lord Michael below
Lord Michael, Lord Michael wherever I go.
I AM, its love protecting here!
I AM, its love protecting here!
I AM, its love protecting here!

Prayer Against Every Evil

Spirit Of Our God, Father, Son , And Holy Spirit,
Most Holy Trinity, Immaculate Virgin Mary,
Angels, Archangels, And Saints Of Heaven,
Descend Upon Us.

Armor of God

Please Purify Us, Lord, Mold Us, Fill Us With Yourself, Use Us.

Banish All The Forces Of Evil From Us, Destroy Them, Vanquish Them, So That We Can Be Healthy And Do Good Deeds.

Banish From Us All Spells, Witchcraft, Black Magic, Malice, Ties, Maledictions, And The Evil Eye; Diabolic Infestations, Oppressions, Possessions; All That Is Evil And Sinful, Jealousy, Perfidy, Envy; Physical, Psychological, Moral, Spiritual, Diabolical Ailments.

Burn All These Evils In Hell, That They May Never Again Touch Me Or Any Other Creature In The Entire World.

I Command And Bid All The Powers Who Molest Me -- By The Power Of God All Powerful, In The Name Of Jesus Christ Our Savior, Through The Intercession Of The Immaculate Virgin Mary -- To Leave Us Forever, And To Be Consigned Into The Everlasting Hell, Where They Will Be Bound By Saint Michael The Archangel, Saint Gabriel, Saint Raphael, our guardian angels, and where they will be crushed under the heel of the Immaculate Virgin Mary.

Armor of God

Prayer for Protection

"Father God, please send your Holy Angels to stand guard over me today (tonight).   I pray that they will minister to me and remind me of your healing power.   Lord please keep me safe from the evil one and strengthen me against all temptations that may come my way. Thank You Lord, in the name of Jesus Christ, I pray, Amen." (based on Psalm 91)

Prayer for Protection

"Lord God, please surround me with favor as with a shield today. Lord, please strengthen your wall of protection around me, keeping me safe from temptation of the flesh, tricks of the Adversary, and all harm.   Lord, please fill my thoughts with Your thoughts and let my words be your words. You are my strength, my shield and my defense, O Lord. Thank You, Lord, in Jesus name I pray, Amen." (based on Psalm 5:12 & Psalm 7:10)

Armor of God

Prayer for Protection

Visit this place, O Lord, and drive far from it all snares of the enemy; let your holy angels dwell with us to preserve us in peace; and let your blessing be upon us always; through Jesus Christ our Lord. Amen.

The almighty and merciful Lord, Father, Son, and Holy Spirit, bless us and keep us. Amen.

Surround Me With Your Light

Surround me with your light, Jesus, and penetrate the very depths of my being with that light. Let there remain no areas of darkness in me or in my family members, but transform our whole being with the healing light of your love. Open me completely to receive your love, Jesus. Thank you for being our family healer and my personal healer.

Armor of God

The Breastplate of St. Patrick

I arise today through a mighty strength, the invocation of the Trinity, through belief in the Threeness, through confession of the Oneness of the Creator of creation.

I arise today through the strength of Christ with His Baptism, through the strength of His Crucifixion with His Burial through the strength of His Resurrection with His Ascension, through the strength of His descent for the Judgment of Doom.

I arise today through the strength of the love of Cherubim in obedience of Angels, in the service of the Archangels, in hope of resurrection to meet with reward, in prayers of Patriarchs, in predictions of Prophets, in preachings of Apostles, in faiths of Confessors, in innocence of Holy Virgins, in deeds of righteous men.

I arise today, through the strength of Heaven: light of Sun, brilliance of Moon, splendor of Fire, speed of Lightning, swiftness of Wind, depth of Sea, stability of Earth, firmness of Rock.

I arise today, through God's strength to pilot me: God's might to uphold me, God's wisdom to guide me, God's eye to look before me, God's ear to hear me, God's word to speak for me, God's hand to guard me, God's way to lie before me, God's shield

Armor of God

to protect me, God's host to secure me:
against snares of devils, against temptations of
vices, against inclinations of nature, against
everyone who shall wish me ill, afar and near, alone
and in a crowd.

I summon today all these powers between me (and
these evils): against every cruel and merciless power
that may oppose my body and my soul, against
incantations of false prophets, against black laws of
heathenry, against false laws of heretics, against
craft of idolatry, against spells of women [any
witch] and smiths and wizards, against every
knowledge that endangers man's body and soul.

Christ to protect me today against poison, against
burning, against drowning, against wounding, so
that there may come abundance of reward.

Christ with me, Christ before me, Christ behind
me, Christ in me, Christ beneath me, Christ above
me, Christ on my right, Christ on my left, Christ in
breadth, Christ in length, Christ in height, Christ in

the heart of every man who thinks of me,
Christ in the mouth of every man who speaks of
me, Christ in every eye that sees me, Christ in every
ear that hears me.

I arise today through a mighty strength, the
invocation of the Trinity, through belief in the

Threeness, through confession of the Oneness of
the Creator of creation. Salvation is of the Lord.
Salvation is of the Lord. Salvation is of Christ. May
Thy Salvation, O Lord, be ever with us.

Christo-Celtic Spell-Prayer Against the Powers of
Darkness *attributed to St. Patrick*

On Terra (earth) in this fateful hour
I place all Heaven with its power
the sun with its brightness
the snow with its whiteness
the fire with all the strength it hath
the lightning with its rapid wrath
the winds with their swiftness along their path
the sea with its deepness
the rocks with their steepness
the earth with it starkness

all these I place

With God's almighty help and grace
between myself and the powers of darkness.
Amen.

Ephesians 6:12-18

12 For our struggle is not against flesh and blood,
but against the rulers, against the authorities,
against the powers of this dark world and against
the spiritual forces of evil in the heavenly realms.

13 Therefore put on the full armor of God, so that
when the day of evil comes, you may be able to
stand your ground, and after you have done
everything, to stand.

14 Stand firm then, with the belt of truth buckled
around your waist, with the breastplate of
righteousness in place,

15 and with your feet fitted with the readiness that
comes from the gospel of peace.

16 In addition to all this, take up the shield of faith, with which you can extinguish all the flaming arrows of the evil one.

17 Take the helmet of salvation and the sword of the Spirit, which is the word of God.

18 And pray in the Spirit on all occasions with all kinds of prayers and requests. With this in mind, be alert and always keep on praying for all the saints.

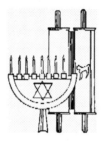

My Help Cometh From HaShem

I will lift up mine eyes unto the mountains: from whence shall my help come?
My help cometh from HaShem, who made heaven and earth.
He will not suffer thy foot to be moved; He that keepeth thee will not slumber.
Behold, He that keepeth Israel doth neither slumber nor sleep.
HaShem is thy keeper; HaShem is thy shade upon

thy right hand.

The sun shall not smite thee by day, nor the moon by night.

HaShem shall keep thee from all evil; He shall keep thy soul.

HaShem shall guard thy going out and thy coming in, from this time forth and for ever.

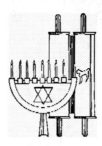

Prayer for Protection

O Lord, grant that this night we may sleep in peace. And that in the morning our awakening may also be in peace. May our daytime be cloaked in your peace.

Protect us and inspire us to think and act only out of love.

Keep far from us all evil; may our paths be free from all obstacles from when we go out until we return home.

Armor of God

I send this prayer to the divine Kuan Yin, and ask humbly for benign and benevolent love and protection. In my time of darkness and need, I am all alone in this world, I feel abandoned and I am scared. I am weak, and I ask for strength. I am sorrowful, and I ask for joy. I am blind, and I ask for sight. I know nothing and ask for wisdom.

Please, Avalokiteshvara, hear my plea, and help me to see what it is I need to see. Guide me in my life and give me your love. I need your religion. I need your love. Help me to live with your example of truthful love and wisdom in my actions.
Though I try, I do not do so well, nor do I try hard enough. I fail and stumble again and again and again. I hurt myself and others in my blind wandering. I know what it is that is good, yet I do bad. Help me, oh great and divine embodiment of compassion to do the right thing.

I put this prayer out to the world for all, and you to see, and kneel before you in supplication and awe. I love you. I need you. Please protect, bless and heal me. I do not wish to ask this of you selfishly, and many more here on Earth need your help as well, but perhaps do not know to call on you. I say this prayer to you for all who may need it as well, and I hope that very soon, we may reap the beneficial reward of your love.

Please help me to find work, and help me to find one with whom I can share an easy love with. In my work, help me to perform it well, and not to endanger my well being with my ego. In love, help me to share with someone all that is good that I have learned, and not to lay upon them the heavyness of my heart and punish her with my love, but to make her glad to be here with me.

Thank you, Kuan Yin, oh great and divine embodiment of compassion-Avalokiteshvara! My love for you is endless, and I give you my eternal thanks for your blessing and protection!

I send this prayer to the divine Kuan Yin, and ask humbly for benign and benevolent love and protection. In my time of darkness and need, I am all alone in this world, I feel abandoned and I am scared. I am weak, and I ask for strength. I am sorrowful, and I ask for joy. I am blind, and I ask for sight. I know nothing and ask for wisdom. Please, Avalokiteshvara, hear my plea, and help me to see what it is I need to see. Guide me in my life and give me your love. I need your religion. I need your love. Help me to live with your example of truthful love and wisdom in my actions.

Though I try, I do not do so well, nor do I try hard enough. I fail and stumble again and again and again. I hurt myself and others in my blind wandering. I know what it is that is good, yet I do bad. Help me, oh great and divine embodiment of compassion to do the right thing.

I put this prayer out to the world for all, and you to see, and kneel before you in supplication and awe. I love you. I need you. Please protect, bless and heal me. I do not wish to ask this of you selfishly, and many more here on Earth need your help as well, but perhaps do not know to call on you. I say this prayer to you for all who may need it as well, and I hope that very soon, we may reap the beneficial reward of your love.

Please help me to find work, and help me to find one with whom I can share an easy love with. In my work, help me to perform it well, and not to endanger my well being with my ego. In love, help me to share with someone all that is good that I have learned, and not to lay upon them the heaviness of my heart and punish her with my love, but to make her glad to be here with me.

Thank you, Kuan Yin, oh great and divine embodiment of compassion-Avalokiteshvara! My love for you is endless, and I give you my eternal thanks for your blessing and protection!

Prayer for Peace and Protection

Kwan Yin of the gentle hands, with arms held wide in benediction: come between my enemies and me and join us together in peace.

Hindu I prostrate myself before the five-faced Lord of Parvati, who is adorned with various ornaments, who shines like the crystal jewel, who is seated peacefully in the lotus pose, with moon-crested crown, with three eyes, wearing trident, thunderbolt, sword and axe on the right side, who holds the serpent, noose, bell, damaru and spear on the left side, and who gives protection from all fear to His devotees.

Shaantam padmaasanastham shashadharamakutam

panchavaktram trinetram,
Shoolam vajram cha khadgam parashumabhayadam
dakshinaange vahantam,
Naagam paasham cha ghantaam damaruka sahitam
chaankusham vaamabhaage,
Naanaalankaara deeptam sphatika maninibham
paarvateesham namaami.

General Prayer

Wielder of the hammer,
red-bearded one,
Thor, protector,
to you I call.
I stand in the midst of a storm
and ask your protection

General Prayer

Thank you, O mighty ones,
for all you have done for me.
May I not forget you, though the world turn against
me.
Though I fall with my enemies rejoicing about me,
it will be your presence that will comfort me,
and I will still thank you for the incomparable
rightness of every moment.

Armor of God

Prayer For Protection

"I dwell in the bright divine light,
All goodness is attracted to me for my highest good.
I am attuned with divine love and divine goodness,
I give thanks for the divine light."

A Prayer and Invocation for Protection and Guidance

Kadoish, kadoish, kadoish, adonai tsebayoth! In the name of the Most High God, Heavenly Father, Divine Mother, and all souls who are 100%aligned with God's unconditionally loving light, I hereby ask to be completely and permanently protected from anything and everything that is not in alignment with my maximum soul growth, happiness, joy, prosperity, perfect health, love, compassion, well-being and peace of mind. I ask for my soul lessons to come to me gently, lovingly and with joy. I am willing to be humble and go within to the Source of my being for guidance. I am willing to see all challenges and difficulties in my life as gifts to help me grow and evolve. I ask for complete and total understanding of what to do, how to think and feel, and how to act in all situations in my life. I ask that I receive wisdom and understanding that are exactly appropriate to share with the people in my life. I ask that I receive exactly what I need from my God Self in order to assist me to be the most loving and compassionate person I can be. I know that the love, wisdom and power of God comes through me in all my relationships. I ask that all negative entities, manifestations of ego, fear, guilt, separation, judgment and anything else that is not in the best interests of me and those around me be dispelled, released, integrated and transcended at this time. I ask that all parts of myself move into alignment with my God Presence. So be it, and so it is. Amen.

5. Spiritual Warfare

Renunciation Of Satan and Claiming the Full Victory

I claim the full victory that my Lord Jesus Christ won on the Cross for me. Having disarmed the powers and authorities, He made a public spectacle of them, triumphing over them by the cross. His victory for me is my victory.

In the name of the Lord Jesus Christ I renounce all the workings of Satan in my life in all its forms, whether brought into my life by my actions or by others. I break all attachments, ground, curses, spells, and rights Satan may have in my life whether such ground was gained through my actions or through others. Strengthened by the intercession of the Immaculate Virgin Mary, Mother of God, of Blessed Michael the Archangel, of the Blessed Apostles Peter and Paul, and all the Saints and Angels of Heaven, and powerful in the holy authority of the name of the Lord Jesus Christ, I ask you Lord to command Satan and all his minions, whomever they may be, to get out of my life and stay out. With that authority I now take back the ground in my life gained by Satan through my sins. I reclaim this ground and my life for Christ. I now dedicate myself to the Lord Jesus Christ; I belong to Him alone. Amen.

<u>Spiritual Warfare Prayer</u>

Heavenly Father, I love You, I praise You, and I worship You. I thank You for sending your Son Jesus Who won victory over sin and death for my salvation. I thank You for sending Your Holy Spirit Who empowers me, guides me, and leads me into fullness of life. I thank You for Mary, my Heavenly

Armor of God

Mother, who intercedes with the holy angels and saints for me.

Lord Jesus Christ, I place myself at the foot of Your cross and ask You to cover me with Your Precious Blood which pours forth from Your Most Sacred Hearth and Your Most Holy Wounds, Cleanse me, my Jesus, in the living water that flows form Your Heart. I ask You to surround me, Lord Jesus, with Your Holy Light.

Heavenly Father, let the healing waters of my baptism now flow back through the maternal and paternal generations to purify my family line of Satan and sin. I come before You, Father, and ask forgiveness for myself, my relatives, and my ancestors, for any calling upon powers that set themselves up in opposition to You or that does not offer true honor to Jesus Christ. In Jesus' Holy Name, I now reclaim any territory that was handed over to Satan and place it under the Lordship of Jesus Christ.

By the power of Your Holy Spirit, reveal to me, Father, any people I need to forgive and any areas of unconfessed sin. Reveal aspects of my life that are not pleasing You, Father, ways that have given or could give Satan a foothold in my life. Father I give to You and unforgiveness; I give to You my sins; and, I give to You all ways that Satan has a hold of my life. Thank You, Father for these revelations, thank You, for Your forgiveness and Your love.

Lord Jesus, in Your Holy Name, I bind all evil spirits of the air, water, ground, underground, and netherworld. I further bind, in Jesus' Name, any and all emissaries of the satanic headquarters and claim the Precious Blood of Jesus on the air, atmosphere, water, ground and their fruits around us, the underground and the netherworld below. Heavenly Father, allow Your Son Jesus to come now with the Holy Spirit, the Blessed Virgin Mary, the holy angels and the saints to protect me from all harm and to keep all evil spirits from taking revenge on me in any way.

(Repeat the following sentence three times; once in honor of the Father, once in honor of the Son, and once in honor of the Holy Spirit.)
In the Holy Name of Jesus, I seal myself, my relatives, this room (place, home, church, car, plane, etc...), and all sources of supply in the Precious Blood of Jesus Christ.

(To break and dissolve all satanic seals, repeat the following paragraph three times in honor of the Holy Trinity because satanic seals are placed three times to blaspheme the Holy Trinity.)
In the Holy Name of Jesus, I break and dissolve any and all curses, hexes, spells, snares, traps, lies, obstacles, deceptions, diversions, spiritual

influences, evil wishes, evil desires, hereditary seals, known and unknown, and every dysfunction and disease from any source including my mistakes and sins.

In Jesus' Name, I dissolve all effects of participation in seances and divination, ouija boards, horoscopes, occult games of all sorts, and any form of worship that does not offer true honor to Jesus Christ.

Holy Spirit, please reveal to me through word of knowledge any evil spirits that have attached themselves to me in any way. (Pause and wait for words to come to you, such as: anger, arrogance, bitterness, brutality, confusion, cruelty, deception, envy, fear, hatred, insecurity, jealousy, pride, resentment, or terror. Pray the following for each of the evil spirits revealed)

In the Name of Jesus, I rebuke you spirit of _____. I command you to go directly to Jesus, without manifestation and without harm to me or anyone, so that He can dispose of

you according to His Holy Will. I thank You, Heavenly Father for Your love. I thank You, Holy Spirit for empowering me to be aggressive against Satan and evil spirits. I thank You, Jesus, for setting me free. I thank you, Mary for interceding for me with the holy angels and the saints.

Armor of God

Lord Jesus fill me with charity, compassion, faith, gentleness, hope, humility, joy, kindness, light, love, mercy, modesty, patience, peace, purity, security, serenity, tranquility, trust, truth, understanding, and wisdom. Help me to walk in Your Light and Truth, illuminated by the Holy Spirit so that together We may praise, honor, and glorify Our Father in time and in eternity. For You, Lord Jesus, are, "...the way, the truth, and the life" (John 14:6 NAB), and You "...have come that we might have life and have it more abundantly" (John 10:10 JB)

"God indeed is my savior; I am confident and unafraid. MY strength and courage is the Lord, and he has been my savior" (Isaiah 12:2 JB). Amen. Alleluia. Amen.

General Prayer

Dear Heavenly Father, I pray this prayer in the power of the HOLY SPIRIT, in the name of JESUS I bind, rebuke and to bring to no effect all division, discord, disunity, strife, anger, wrath murder, criticism, condemnation, pride, envy, jealousy, gossip, slander, evil speaking, complaining, lying, false teaching, false gifts, false manifestations, lying signs and wonders, poverty, fear spirits and spirits of antichrist.

General Prayer

I am a child of GOD! I resist the devil! No weapon formed against me shall prosper! I put on the whole armor of GOD. I take authority over this day, in JESUS NAME!! Let it be prosperous for me and let me walk in your love LORD.

General Prayer

The HOLY SPIRIT leads and guides me today. I discern between the righteous and the wicked. I take authority over Satan and all of his demons, and those people who are influenced by them. I declare Satan is under my feet and shall remain there all day. I am the righteous of GOD through CHRIST JESUS. I am GOD`S property! Satan you are bound from my family, my mind, my body, my home, my friends and my finances. I confess that I am healed and whole. I flourish, I am long lived, I am stable, durable, incorruptible, fruitful, virtuous, full of peace, patience and love. Whatsoever I set my hands to do shall prosper, for GOD supplies all of my needs. I have all authority over Satan, all demons and beasts of the field.

General Prayer

"Father God, I ask that You will send Your forces out to drive back the enemies of Christ that are working in this situation. Your Word says that the adversaries of the Lord shall be broken in pieces; from heaven He will thunder against them. Lord, I pray that you would break your enemies in pieces in Your perfect timing, and bring salvation, restoration and healing to all people who are involved."

Armor of God

General Prayer

"Lord God, I ask you to move against the forces of evil. I invite You to act in Your mighty power in this situation. Throw the enemy forces into confusion and frustrate their counsel. I pray that they will not prosper in all their schemes of rebellion against You and Your people. I pray that the financial support of these evildoers will erode away as long as they do evil in Your sight. I pray that You will turn their hearts to Yourself and draw them unto Your salvation in Jesus Christ. Thank You Father. In Jesus Christ, Amen"

General Prayer

"Heavenly Father, I ask that you would unmask the enemy's deception over these people who are rebelling against you in doing this evil. Lord God, please stretch out Your mighty hand against their schemes and thwart their every move. Please draw each of them to salvation in Jesus Christ. Thank You Father. In Jesus Christ, Amen"

General Prayer

"Lord God almighty, You are the Lord of hosts, the Commander of the armies of heaven, the Most High God. I pray that you will thunder from heaven against the forces of darkness that are working in this situation. Lord, may you utter Your voice, sending hailstones and coals of fire into the enemy's camp. Lord, send out Your arrows and scatter the foe with lightning in abundance. Vanquish Your enemies, O God and rebuke them with the blast of Your holy breath. To You alone be all glory, honor and praise forever. In Jesus Christ I pray, Amen."

A Spiritual Warrior's Prayer

"Almighty and most merciful Father, we humbly beseech Thee, of Thy great goodness, to restrain the forces that would seek our destruction. Grant us the courage and wisdom to do Battle for Thy greater glory and not for our own. Graciously hearken to us as Thy soldiers who call upon Thee, that armed with Thy power and love and with the Sword of Thy Spirit, we may advance from victory to victory and crush the oppression and wickedness of our enemies. With our Blessed Mother help us oh Lord to crush the head of Satan and to establish Thy justice and love among men and nations. Amen."

Prayer Against Fear

O Father...my Father in heaven, what time I am afraid I will trust in You. Father, forgive me for giving into the fear of this situation. Forgive me for focusing on the problem rather than on You, the Problem Solver. And especially, Father, forgive me for forgetting that everything that happens in this life does so to bring us into a closer relationship with You.

You Word in James 1:2 says we should "count it all joy when various trials and problems enter our lives, because they are for the testing of our faith." But Father, that is so hard to do! Please help me to trust that You know what You are doing in allowing this trial to occur in my life.

I choose to turn this whole situation over to You.
Your Word in Proverbs 21:1 says, 'The king's heart
is in the hand of the LORD; like the rivers of water
He (that is You, Father) turns it wherever He
wishes." Father, I do trust You, and I know You
will work everything to good in Your time.
By faith, Father, I push back the curtain of fear
Satan's evil hosts have enclosed me in and claim
Your 'fear not' promises in Isaiah 41:10 and 2
Timothy 1:7.

I praise You for Your love and mercy to me and
my family. I praise You that Satan and all his
cohorts are dead meat because of Your grace.

Thank You, Father, for not giving up on us even
when our faith falters and falls. I leave this situation
in Your capable hands to do 'whatever...whatever
You allow into my life or my family's lives, because
I know You are powerful and strong enough to get
us through it.' In JESUS' name, Amen.

General Prayer

From the snares of the devil, deliver us, O Lord.
That Thy Church may serve Thee in peace and

liberty, we beseech Thee to hear us. That Thou may crush down all enemies of Thy Church, we beseech Thee to hear us.

(Holy water is sprinkled in the place where you may be.)

The Blood of Jesus Christ

"Lord, I cover myself and everyone around me with the blood of Jesus. I cover all of the members of my family (call them by name) with the blood of Jesus. I cover my home, my land, my car, my finances, my marriage, my ministry, with the blood of Jesus. In the Name of Jesus Christ, by the power of His blood, I break off every power of the kingdom of darkness and cancel every argument in heaven that has established itself against the plans of God in my life and spoil every attack of the enemy. I call forth, in the name of Jesus, all of God's plans and purposes for my life, and my family. As for me and my house, we shall serve the Lord. Satan, the blood of Jesus is against you and you have no authority over my life. NO WEAPON FORMED AGAINST ME (OR MY FAMILY) SHALL PROSPER!"

<u>Asking God to move against Satan and other evil forces:</u>

"Father God, I ask that You will send Your forces out to drive back the enemies of Christ that are working in this situation.   Your Word says that the adversaries of the Lord shall be broken in pieces; from heaven He will thunder against them. Lord, I pray that you would break your enemies in pieces in Your perfect timing, and bring salvation, restoration and healing to all people who are involved."   (Based on 1 Samuel 2:10)

"To You, O Lord, I lift up my soul. O my God, I trust in You; let me not be ashamed; Let not my enemies triumph over me. Consider my enemies, for they are many; and they hate me with cruel hatred. Keep my soul, and deliver me; let me not be ashamed for I put my trust in You. In Jesus Christ, Amen" (based on Psalm 25:1-2, 19-20 NKJV)

"Plead my cause, O Lord, with those who strive with me; fight against those who fight against me. Take hold of shield and buckler, and stand up for my help. Also draw out the spear and stop those who pursue me. Say to my soul, "I am your salvation." Let those be put to shame and brought to dishonor who seek after my life; let those be turned back and brought to confusion who plot my hurt. Let them be like chaff before the wind, and let the angel of the Lord chase them. Let their way be dark and slippery, and let the angel of the Lord pursue them. In Jesus Christ, Amen" (based on Psalm 35:16 NKJV)

"Lord God, I ask you to move against the forces of evil. I invite You to act in Your mighty power in this situation. Throw the enemy forces into confusion and frustrate their counsel. I pray that they will not prosper in all their schemes of rebellion against You and Your people. I pray that the financial support of these evildoers will erode away as long as they do evil in Your sight. I pray that You will turn their hearts to Yourself and draw them unto Your salvation in Jesus Christ.

Thank You Father. In Jesus Christ, Amen"

Armor of God

General Prayer

"Heavenly Father, I ask that you would unmask the enemy's deception over these people who are rebelling against you in doing this evil. Lord God, please stretch out Your mighty hand against their schemes and thwart their every move. Please draw each of them to salvation in Jesus Christ. Thank You Father. In Jesus Christ, Amen"

Binding Prayer

"Father in heaven, I stand in faith on the authority I have as a believer in Jesus Christ, and a co-heir to his kingdom. In the name of Jesus Christ, I bind every evil spirit and every evil plan made in this situation. I cancel the enemy's plans and call forth God's plans for this situation. God's word says that God has plans for good and not evil for us and I claim those plans now. Father, I ask that your will be done in this situation, as it is done in heaven. I give thanks and praise to you. In Jesus' name I pray, Amen."

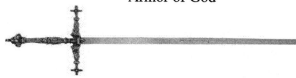

<u>Simple Binding Prayer:</u>
"Father God, I thank you for sending your Son
Jesus to die for me, and resurrecting him to sit at
your right hand in Heaven right now.   I thank you
for bestowing upon Him all power and authority
over evil.   In the name of Jesus Christ, I speak to
any evil spirits, [specially spirits of *_____
(fill in the blank)] I bind you from attacking me
now and throughout this day. Leave me now and
go straight to Jesus Christ who will deal with you. I
am covered and protected by the blood of Jesus
Christ. Amen."

<u>Supplication Against Satan</u>

O God,
we seek refuge in Thee

71

from the instigations of the accursed Satan,
his trickery, and his traps,
from trust in his false hopes, his promises,
his delusions, and his snares,
and lest he should make himself crave
to lead us away from Thy obedience
and to degrade us through our disobeying Thee,
and lest what he has shown us as beautiful be
beautiful for us
and what he has shown us as detestable weigh
down upon us.
O God,
drive him away from us through Thy worship,
throw him down through our perseverance in Thy
love, and place between him and us a covering
that he cannot tear away
and a solid barrier that he cannot cut through!
O God,
bless Muhammad and his Household,
distract Satan from us with some of Thy enemies,
preserve us from him through Thy good guarding,
spare us his treachery,
turn his back toward us,
and cut off from us his trace!
O God,
bless Muhammad and his Household,
give us to enjoy guidance
the like of his misguidance,
increase us in piety
against his seduction,

and make us walk in reverential fear
contrary to his path of ruin!
O God,
assign him no place of entrance into our hearts
and do not allow him to make his home in that
which is with us!
O God,
cause us to recognize the falsehood with which he
tempts us,
and once Thou hast caused us to recognize it,
protect us from it!
Make us see what will allow us to outwit him,
inspire us with all that we can make ready for him,
awaken us from the heedless slumber of relying
upon him,
and help us well, through Thy giving success,
against him!
O God,
saturate our hearts with the rejection of his works
and be gentle to us by destroying his stratagems!
O God,
bless Muhammad and his Household,
turn his authority away from us,
cut off his hope from us,
and keep him from craving for us!
O God,
bless Muhammad and his Household,
and place our fathers, our mothers,
our children, our wives,
our siblings, our relatives,
and the faithful among our neighbors,

male and female,
in a sanctuary impregnable to him,
a guarding fortress,
a defending cave!
Clothe them in shields protective against him
and give them arms that will cut him down!
O God,
include in that everyone who
witnesses to Thee as Lord,
devotes himself sincerely to Thy Unity,
shows enmity toward him
through the reality of servanthood,
and seeks help from Thee against him
through knowledge of the divine sciences!
O God,
undo what he ties,
unstitch what he sews up,
dislocate what he devises,
frustrate him when he makes up his mind,
and destroy what he establishes!
O God,
rout his troops,
nullify his trickery,
make his cave collapse,
and rub his nose in the ground!
O God,
place us in the ranks of his enemies
and remove us from the number of his friends,
that we obey him not when he entices us
and answer him not when he calls to us!

Armor of God

We command everyone who obeys our command
to be his enemy
and we admonish everyone who follows our
prohibition
not to follow him!
O God,
bless Muhammad,
the Seal of the prophets and lord of the emissaries,
and the folk of his house,
the good, the pure!
Give refuge to us, our families, our brothers,
and all the faithful, male and female,
from that from which we seek refuge,
and grant us sanctuary from that through fear of
which
we seek sanctuary in Thee!
Hear our supplication to Thee,
bestow upon us that of which we have been
heedless,
and safeguard for us what we have forgotten!
Through all this bring us into the ranks of the
righteous
and the degrees of the faithful!
Amen, Lord of the worlds!

Invocation for Action Against the Dark Forces

Oh, living light of love.
Oh, great and Holy Divine Mother
That IS the sweetness of life itself,

Come, come, come
Into the Earth plane as never before.
Come, O dear Cosmic Mother!
Enfold us all.
Take us all into your wondrous embrace.
Comfort us and give us the strength
And the bravery to be who we truly are -
Beings of Love, Forgiveness, Joy, and Laughter.

And, O Divine Mother,
Bring your broom and sweep clean the earth
Of all those who do not respect thee,
Of all those misguided children,
For they are your children as well,

Armor of God

Who have foolishly taken the Dark Path

Of domination, oppression, and the
Unbalanced manifestations of masculine energy.
Let the Feminine Ray arise!
Let the Feminine Ray be glorified.
Let the Feminine Ray come into ultimate power.
And may there be, now,
A very powerful Karmic readjustment on this
planet,
On earth as it is in Heaven.
That all those who want to dominate others
Who want to oppress others,
Who want to punish others,
Who tend towards cruelty, malice, torture,
And all forms of such evil-doing,
Let these know the just judgment
Of the Lord God and his Minions of Light.
Let the Great Archangel Michael
Now swoop onto the earth

Bringing his numberless legions of angels
And wipe clean the earth
Of those who will not stop in their fighting
In their terrorism of others
And in their lies toward their brethren.
Let all the layers of Darkness be exposed
To the fullest light of truth.
And let all world leaders who are inclined to war,
Who are inclined to collaborate with those dark
forces That up to this point have controlled

Armor of God

The money and the power on this planet,
Let these be given a choice.
Dispatch Angels to them as they sleep,
Bright messengers that will awaken them
And say to them "You, who head the country,
Be AWARE.
The CHOICE is upon you now:
Shall you continue to be in the camp of these Dark
Ones, That would war and take and lie and kill?
For if so, you shall go down with them as well,
And quickly at that!
If you have the heart,
If you have the mind,
To see that this is not
The way of Light, Love, and Joy
And have the bravery to change your stance,
Do something of true worth for your country,
Then you will be a leader, indeed.
Otherwise, prepare to lose all that you have.
And that will, in all likelihood,
Include your physical life as well.
For there can be no further toleration
Of that Evil which delights in malice.

Now let the avalanche of Karma
Be released upon all those
Who will not even for the moment
Consider changing their hard-hearted
And hard-headed attitudes.

Armor of God

And may these be returned to the Spirit Realm
For they can be educated and re-programmed
For such things do not work,
Never have worked
And never shall work.
O Divine Mother, come personally.
Touch our hearts.
Enlighten us all that we might see
That TOLERANCE is beautiful.
But it does no good
When it is expended upon those
Who have no tolerance for anyone but themselves.
Let now the Lords of Karma
Move mightily and swiftly
And stop these who would
Perpetrate only further warfare
And manipulations of this population.
We call for the All Seeing Eye of God
To expose them on the media,
In front of everyone;
We call for the All Seeing Eye of God
To expose the sham that they are behind.

The facade that they have created
And all of that which occurred
Upon the 11th of September
Of the Year 2001
Which was not what it was portrayed to be.
Let there be an exposure now
From the very depths.
Let them ALL be shown

Armor of God

For precisely who and what they are --
Perpetrators of lies.
Those who are the reincarnated
Sons of Belial of Atlantis
And those who have come here from other planets
And have simply been handed the reins
By the so-called leaders of the countries of the
earth plane.
Let there now be a sorting and a sifting,
Guided and directed by
The Great and Holy Master Jesus himself.
Let him bring his mighty sword and sever ties,
If necessary, familial ties,
That keep the truly sweet, forgiving, and innocent
bound
To those who are inclined and prone to
Dominate, harm, lie, cheat, steal, oppress,
And do all those things
Which have nothing to do with the Christ.
And may the Great Lord Buddha,
Lord of the World also be ensconced in full glory,
Radiating his Golden Light of Wisdom
So that ALL rise and see clearly
How they have been lied to.

How they have been foolish
In trusting such as these!
How they need to have questioned
Authority wherever they found it!
And only when they could hear

Armor of God

Truth ringing in their own hearts

Would they have been justified
In being satisfied with such as these.
Let God's will be done in all matters,
And let the Judgment be swift,
Specifically upon all those who align themselves
With institutions such as the IRS
Which unjustly take monies
From those who need it most.
Let their charge now be this:
That we, the People of Earth,
NOW do charge institutions such as the IRS
With stealing food out of the mouths of children
who need it,
With stealing food from the elderly
And those who cannot work,
And using it to create war and war-like machines.
We DEMAND that they be
Brought to account this very hour,
That they all be held accountable
For every drop of blood
For which they are responsible
And for every war they have ever instigated
Simply to generate money.
Let the Living God Almighty
Within each one of us RISE up as never before.
And be UNITED as a wall of fire
That burns, burns, burns
Right through their façade,
Right through their compounds,

Armor of God

Melting their computers,
Causing them, each one, to go running in fear.
For At Last,
The Lord of Righteousness
Is upon the doorstep
And demanding explanation
For their evil deeds and actions.
We will not tolerate it for one more second.
We demand Justice now.
Let them be the ones who are on the run and not
we.
Let them be the ones who are now scattering,
Running to so many peaks,
Hiding from the ones
Who would bring them to their just end.
Let these things occur,
Now and forever more
Until the planet is as it was always meant to be:
A Garden of Beauty, a place of Love, Joy,
That *terra* might join her sisters and brothers
In the cosmic parade of planets liberated.
And may the Great and Holy Master Saint
Germain,
The Lord of Freedom for the Earth,
Hurl his mighty Miracle Pouch into the
governments
Of every single country that currently exists.
And consume with the Violet Flame all of that
which is unrighteous,
Its causes, its cores, its seeds, its effects
And all its memories connected therewith.

Armor of God

Let God's will be done.
Let the Light of Freedom alone guide
This wondrous parade of light.
And may the Lords of Karma answer our call.
And once and for all bring us back to Love, Love,
Love, and Love
So be it forever more.
Amen

6. Prayers to Archangel Michael

Michael the Archangel, whose name means "who is like God" is the "leader" of the Archangels. He is the Archangel who led the loyal Angels against Lucifer and cast him out of Heaven. He is considered the greatest Angel of all in Christianity, Islam and Judaism. He is the patron Saint of Policemen. He is also referenced and called upon in many Christian and non-Christian prayers, especially those prayers asking for protection or intervention against evil. He is also called upon in many versions of exorcism rite. The prayers to

Armor of God

Archangel Michael are among to most powerful and useful for protection against evil spirits.

This is the most common version of a prayer for protection that is easy to memorize and can be used at anytime.

Michael the Archangel, defend us in battle; be our safeguard against the wickedness and snares of the devil. May God rebuke him, we humbly pray. And do you, O prince of the heavenly host, by the power of God, cast into Hell Satan and all the evil spirits who prowl about the world seeking the ruin of souls. Amen.

Help Against Spiritual Enemies

Glorious St. Michael, Prince of the heavenly hosts, who standest always ready to give assistance to the people of God; who didst fight with the dragon, the old serpent, and didst cast him out of heaven, and now valiantly defendest the Church of God that the gates of hell may never prevail against her, I earnestly entreat thee to assist me also, in the painful and dangerous conflict which I have to sustain against the same formidible foe. Be with me, O mighty Prince! that I may courageously fight and wholly vanquish that proud spirit, whom thou hast by the Divine Power, so gloriously overthrown, and whom our powerful King, Jesus Christ, has, in our nature, so completely overcome; to the end that having triumphed over the enemy of my salvation, I may with thee and the holy angels, praise the clemency of God who, having refused mercy to the rebellious angels after their fall, has granted repentance and forgiveness to fallen man. Amen.

Saint Michael Powerful Aid
Glorious Prince of the heavenly hosts and victor over rebellious spirits, be mindful of me who am so weak and sinful and yet so prone to pride and ambition. Lend me, I pray, thy powerful aid in every temptation and difficulty, and above all do not forsake me in my last struggle with the powers of evil. Amen.

Armor of God

Saint Michael, for Personal Protection

Saint Michael, the Archangel! Glorious Prince, chief and champion of the heavenly hosts; guardian of the souls of men; conqueror of the rebel angels! How beautiful art thou, in thy heaven-made armor. We love thee, dear Prince of Heaven!
We, thy happy clients, yearn to enjoy thy special protection. Obtain for us from God a share of thy sturdy courage; pray that we may have a strong and tender love for our Redeemer and, in every danger or temptation, be invincible against the enemy of our souls. O standard-bearer of our salvation! Be with us in our last moments and when our souls quit this earthly exile, carry them safely to the judgment seat of Christ, and may Our Lord and Master bid thee bear us speedily to the kingdom of eternal bliss. Teach us ever to repeat the sublime cry: "Who is like unto God?" Amen.

Most glorious Prince of the Heavenly Armies, Saint Michael the Archangel, defend us in "our battle against principalities and powers, against the rulers of this world of darkness, against the spirits of wickedness in the high places" (Ephes., VI, 12). Come to the assistance of men who God has created to His likeness and whom He has redeemed at a great price from the tyranny of the devil. Holy Church venerates thee as her guardian and protector; to thee, the Lord has entrusted the souls of the redeemed to be led into heaven. Pray therefore the God of Peace to crush Satan beneath our feet, that he may no longer retain men captive and do injury to the Church. Offer our prayers to the Most High, that without delay they may draw His mercy down upon us; take hold of "the dragon, the old serpent, which is the devil and Satan", bind him and cast him into the bottomless pit "so that he may no longer seduce the nations"

Armor of God

Written by Pope Leo XIII, 1888

O Glorious Archangel St. Michael, Prince of the heavenly host, be our defense in the terrible warfare which we carry on against principalities and powers, against the rulers of this world of darkness, and spirits of evil. Come to the aid of man, whom God created immortal, made in His own image and likeness, and redeemed at a great price from the tyranny of the devil. Fight this day the battle of the Lord, together with the holy angels, as already thou hast fought the leader of the proud angels, Lucifer, and his apostate host, who were powerless to resist Thee, nor was there place for them any longer in heaven. That cruel, that ancient serpent, who is called the devil or Satan, who seduces the whole world, was cast into the abyss with his angels.

Behold, this primeval enemy and slayer of men has taken courage. Transformed into an angel of light, he wanders about with all the multitude of wicked spirits, invading the earth in order to blot out the name of God and of His Christ, to seize upon, slay and cast into eternal perdition souls destined for the crown of eternal glory. This wicked dragon pours out, as a most impure flood, the venom of his malice on men; his depraved mind, corrupt heart, his spirit of lying, impiety, blasphemy, his pestilential breath of impurity and of every vice and iniquity. These most crafty enemies have filled and inebriated with gall and bitterness the Church, the Spouse of the Immaculate Lamb, and have laid impious hands on her most sacred possessions. In the Holy Place itself, where has been set up the See of the most holy Peter and the Chair of Truth for the light of the world, they have raised the throne of their abominable impiety, with the iniquitous design that when the Pastor has been struck, the sheep may be scattered.

Arise then, O invincible Prince, bring help against the attacks of the lost spirits to the people of God, and give them the victory. They venerate Thee as their protector and patron; in Thee Holy Church glories as her defense against the malicious power of hell; to Thee has God entrusted the souls of men to be established in heavenly beatitude. Oh, pray to the God of peace that He may put Satan under our feet, so far conquered that he may no longer be able to hold men in captivity and harm the Church. Offer our prayers in the sight of the Most High, so that they may quickly conciliate the mercies of the Lord; and beating down the dragon, the ancient serpent who is the devil and Satan, do Thou again make him captive in the abyss, that he may no longer seduce the nations. Amen.

V. Behold the Cross of the Lord; be scattered, hostile powers.

R. The Lion of the tribe of Judah has conquered, the root of David.

V. Let Thy mercies be upon us, O Lord

R. As we have hoped in Thee.

V. O Lord, hear my prayer.

R. And let my cry come unto Thee

LET US PRAY

God, the Father of our Lord Jesus Christ, we call upon Thy holy name, and we humbly implore Thy clemency, that by the intercession of Mary, ever Virgin Immaculate and our Mother, and of the glorious Archangel St. Michael, Thou wouldst deign to help us against Satan and all other unclean spirits, who wander about the world for the injury of the human race and the ruin of souls. Amen.

7. Exorcism

An exorcism is merely a clearing out of a bad or evil spirit. In most cases it is not as dramatic as Hollywood would have you believe but there are times when there is a real tug of war going on over a person. These prayers should not be used unless it is necessary and you are willing to take the risks involved with confronting a negative entity.

This is a short version of a Christian Exorcism that can be said by a regular person or a Priest.

In the Name of Jesus Christ, our God and Lord, strengthened by the intercession of the Immaculate Virgin Mary, Mother of God, of Blessed Michael the Archangel, of the Blessed Apostles Peter and Paul and all the Saints. (and powerful in the holy authority of our ministry)(Lay people omit this parenthesis), we confidently undertake to repulse the attacks and deceits of the devil.

Armor of God

PSALM 68God arises; His enemies are scattered and those who hate Him flee before Him. As smoke is driven away, so are they driven; as wax melts before the fire, so the wicked perish at the presence of God.

V. Behold the Cross of the Lord, flee bands of enemies.

R. He has conquered, the Lion of the tribe of Juda, the offspring of David.

V. May thy mercy, Lord, descend upon us.

R. As great as our hope in Thee.

(The crosses indicate a blessing to be given if a priest recites the Exorcism; if a lay person recites it, they indicate the Sign of the Cross to be made silently by that person.)

We drive you from us, whoever you may be, unclean spirits, all satanic powers, all infernal invaders, all wicked legions, assemblies and sects; in the Name and by the power of Our Lord Jesus Christ, + may you be snatched away and driven from the Church of God and from the souls made to the image and likeness of God and redeemed by the Precious Blood of the Divine Lamb. + Most cunning serpent, you shall no more dare to deceive the human race, persecute the Church, torment God's elect and sift them as wheat. + The Most High God commands you. + He with whom in great insolence, you still claim to be equal; "He who wants all men to be saved and to come to the knowledge of the truth" (1 Tim., 11, 4). God the Father commands you. +God the Son commands you. +God the Holy Ghost commands you.

+Christ, God's Word made flesh, commands you; + He who to save our race outdone through you envy, "humbled Himself, becoming obedient even unto death" (Phil., 11,8); He who had built His Church on the firm rock and declared that the gates of hell shall not prevail against Her, because He will dwell with Her "all days even to the end of the world" (St. Mat., XXVIII, 20). The sacred Sign of the Cross commands you, + as does the power of the mysteries of the Christian Faith. + The glorious Mother of God; the Virgin Mary, commands you; + She who by her humility and from the first moment of her Immaculate Conception, crushed your proud head. The faith of the Holy Apostles Peter and Paul and of the other Apostles commands you. + The blood of the Martyrs and the pious intercession of all the Saints commands you. + Thus, cursed dragon, and you, diabolical legions, we adjure you by the living God, + by the true God, + by the holy God, + by the God "who so loved the world that He gave His only Son, that every soul believing in Him might not perish but have life everlasting" (St. John, III);

stop deceiving human creatures and pouring out to
them the poison of eternal damnation; stop
harming the Church and hindering her liberty. Be
gone, Satan, inventor and master of all deceit,
enemy of man's salvation. Give place to Christ in
whom you have found none of your works; give
place to the One, Holy, Catholic and Apostolic
Church acquired by Christ at the price of His
Blood. Stoop beneath the all-powerful Hand of
God; tremble and flee when we invoke
the Holy and terrible Name of Jesus, this Name
which causes hell to tremble, this Name to which
the Virtues, Powers and Dominations of
heaven are humbly submissive, this Name which
the Cherubim and Seraphim praise unceasingly
repeating: Holy, Holy, Holy is the Lord, the
God of Armies.

V. O Lord, hear my prayer.

R. And let my cry come unto Thee.

V. May the Lord be with thee.

R. And with thy spirit.

Let us pray. God of heaven God of earth, God of
Angels, God of Archangels, God of Patriarchs,
God of Prophets, God of Apostles, God of
Martyrs, God of Confessors, God of Virgins, God
who has power to give life after death and rest after

work, because there is no other God than Thee and there can be no other, for Thou art the Creator of all things, visible and invisible, of whose reign there shall be no end, we humbly prostrate ourselves before Thy glorious Majesty and we beseech Thee to deliver us by Thy power from all the tyranny of the infernal spirits, from their snares, their lies and their furious wickedness; deign, O

Lord, to grant us Thy powerful protection and to keep us safe and sound. We beseech Thee through Jesus Christ Our Lord. Amen.

First Part of the Glorious St. Michael's Exorcism

Pope Leo XIII had a vision of Angels in Battles and he wrote this afterwards.

Armor of God

O glorious Prince of the heavenly host, St. Michael, the Archangel, defend us in the battle and in the fearful warfare that we are waging against the principalities and powers, against the rulers of this world of darkness, against the evil spirits. Come thou to the assistance of men, whom Almighty God created immortal, making them in His own image and likeness and redeeming them at a great price from the tyranny of Satan.

Fight this day the battle of the Lord with thy legions of holy Angels, even as of old thou didst fight against Lucifer, the leader of the proud spirits and all his rebel angels, who were powerless to stand against thee, neither was their place found any more in heaven. And that apostate angel, transformed into an angel of darkness who still creeps about the earth to encompass our ruin, was cast headlong into the abyss together with his followers. But behold, that first enemy of mankind, and a murderer from the beginning, has regained his confidence. Changing himself into an angel of light, he goes about with the whole multitude of the wicked spirits to invade the earth and blot out the name of God and of His Christ, to plunder, to slay and to consign to eternal damnation the souls that have been destined for a crown of everlasting life. This wicked serpent, like an unclean torrent, pours into men of depraved minds and corrupt hearts the poison of his malice, the spirit of lying, impiety and blasphemy, and the deadly breath of impurity and every form of vice and iniquity. These crafty enemies of mankind have filled to overflowing with gall and wormwood the Church, which is the Bride of the lamb without spot; they have laid profane hands upon her most sacred treasures.

Make haste, therefore, O invincible Prince, to help the people of God against the inroads of the lost spirits and grant us the victory. Amen.

The Roman Ritual for Exorcism

This is the translated text from the 1954 version of the Catholic Exorcism.

Part XIII. Exorcism

Chapter I: General Rules Concerning Exorcism

1. A priest--one who is expressly and particularly authorized by the Ordinary--when he intends to

perform an exorcism over persons tormented by the devil, must be properly distinguished for his piety, prudence, and integrity of life. He should fulfill this devout undertaking in all constancy and humility, being utterly immune to any striving for human aggrandizement, and relying, not on his own, but on the divine power. Moreover, he ought to be of mature years, and revered not alone for his office but for his moral qualities.

2. In order to exercise his ministry rightly, he should resort to a great deal more study of the matter (which has to be passed over here for the sake of brevity), by examining approved authors and cases from experience; on the other hand, let him carefully observe the few more important points enumerated here.

3. Especially, he should not believe too readily that a person is possessed by an evil spirit; but he ought to ascertain the signs by which a person possessed can be distinguished from one who is suffering from some illness, especially one of a psychological nature.[1] Signs of possession may be the following: ability to speak with some facility in a strange tongue or to understand it when spoken by another; the faculty of divulging future and hidden events; display of powers which are beyond the subject's age and natural condition; and various other indications which, when taken together as a whole, build up the evidence.

4. In order to understand these matters better, let him inquire of the person possessed, following one or the other act of exorcism, what the latter experienced in his body or soul while the exorcism was being performed, and to learn also what particular words in the form had a more intimidating effect upon the devil, so that hereafter these words may be employed with greater stress and frequency.

5. He will be on his guard against the arts and subterfuges which the evil spirits are wont to use in deceiving the exorcist. For oft times they give deceptive answers and make it difficult to understand them, so that the exorcist might tire and give up, or so it might appear that the afflicted one is in no wise possessed by the devil.

6. Once in a while, after they are already recognized, they conceal themselves and leave the body practically free from every molestation, so that the victim believes himself completely delivered. Yet the exorcist may not desist until he sees the signs of deliverance.

7. At times, moreover, the evil spirits place whatever obstacles they can in the way, so that the patient may not submit to exorcism, or they try to convince him that his affliction is a natural one. Meanwhile, during the exorcism, they cause him to

fall asleep, and dangle some illusion before him, while they seclude themselves, so that the afflicted one appears to be freed.

8. Some reveal a crime which has been committed and the perpetrators thereof, as well as the means of putting an end to it. Yet the afflicted person must beware of having recourse on this account to sorcerers or necromancers or to any parties except the ministers of the Church, or of making use of any superstitious or forbidden practice.

9. Sometimes the devil will leave the possessed person in peace and even allow him to receive the holy Eucharist, to make it appear that he has departed. In fact, the arts and frauds of the evil one for deceiving a man are innumerable. For this reason the exorcist must be on his guard not to fall into this trap.

10. Therefore, he will be mindful of the words of our Lord (Mt 17.20), to the effect that there is a certain type of evil spirit who cannot be driven out except by prayer and fasting. Therefore let him avail himself of these two means above all for imploring the divine assistance in expelling demons, after the example of the holy fathers; and not only himself, but let him induce others, as far as possible, to do the same.

11. If it can be done conveniently the possessed person should be led to church or to some other sacred and worthy place, where the exorcism will be held, away from the crowd. But if the person is ill, or for any valid reason, the exorcism may take place in a private home.

12. The subject, if in good mental and physical health, should be exhorted to implore God's help, to fast, and to fortify himself by frequent reception of penance and holy communion, at the discretion of the priest. And in the course of the exorcism he should be fully recollected, with his intention fixed on God, whom he should entreat with firm faith and in all humility. And if he is all the more grievously tormented, he ought to bear this patiently, never doubting the divine assistance.

13. He ought to have a crucifix at hand or somewhere in sight. If relics of the saints are available, they are to be applied in a reverent way to the breast or the head of the person possessed (the relics must be properly and securely encased and covered). One will see to it that these sacred objects are not treated improperly or that no injury is done them by the evil spirit. However, one should not hold the holy Eucharist over the head of the person or in any way apply it to his body, owing to the danger of desecration.

14. The exorcist must not digress into senseless prattle nor ask superfluous questions or such as are prompted by curiosity, particularly if they pertain to future and hidden matters, all of which have nothing to do with his office. Instead, he will bid the unclean spirit keep silence and answer only when asked. Neither ought he to give any credence to the devil if the latter maintains that he is the spirit of some saint or of a deceased party, or even claims to be a good angel.

15. But necessary questions are, for example: the number and name of the spirits inhabiting the patient, the time when they entered into him, the cause thereof, and the like. As for all jesting, laughing, and nonsense on the part of the evil spirit--the exorcist should prevent it or contemn it, and he will exhort the bystanders (whose number must be very limited) to pay no attention to such goings on; neither are they to put any question to the subject. Rather they should intercede for him to God in all humility and urgency.

16. Let the priest pronounce the exorcism in a commanding and authoritative voice, and at the same time with great confidence, humility, and fervor; and when he sees that the spirit is sorely vexed, then he oppresses and threatens all the more. If he notices that the person afflicted is experiencing a disturbance in some part of his body

or an acute pain or a swelling appears in some part,
he traces the sign of the cross over that place
and sprinkles it with holy water, which he must
have at hand for this purpose.

17. He will pay attention as to what words in
particular cause the evil spirits to tremble, repeating
them the more frequently. And when he comes to a
threatening expression, he recurs to it again and
again, always increasing the punishment. If he
perceives that he is making progress, let him persist
for two, three, four hours, and longer if he can,
until victory is attained.

18. The exorcist should guard against giving or
recommending any medicine to the patient, but
should leave this care to physicians.

19. While performing the exorcism over a woman,
he ought always to have assisting him several
women of good repute, who will hold on to the
person when she is harassed by the evil spirit.
These assistants ought if possible to be close
relatives of the subject and for the sake of decency
the exorcist will avoid saying or doing anything
which might prove an occasion of evil thoughts to
himself or to the others.

20. During the exorcism he shall preferably employ
words from Holy Writ, rather than forms of his

own or of someone else. He shall, moreover, command the devil to tell whether he is detained in that body by necromancy, by evil signs or amulets; and if the one possessed has taken the latter by mouth, he should be made to vomit them; if he has them concealed on his person, he should expose them; and when discovered they must be burned. Moreover, the person should be exhorted to reveal all his temptations to the exorcist.

21. Finally, after the possessed one has been freed, let him be admonished to guard himself carefully against falling into sin, so as to afford no opportunity to the evil spirit of returning, lest the last state of that man become worse than the former.

Endnotes

1. From the emended text of the 1952 edition.

Chapter II: Rite For Exorcism

1. The priest delegated by the Ordinary to perform this office should first go to confession or at least elicit an act of contrition, and, if convenient, offer the holy Sacrifice of the Mass, and implore God's help in other fervent prayers. He vests in surplice and purple stole. Having before him the person possessed (who should be bound if there is any danger), he traces the sign of the cross over him,

over himself, and the bystanders, and then sprinkles all of them with holy water. After this he kneels and says the Litany of the Saints, exclusive of the prayers which follow it. All present are to make the responses. At the end of the litany he adds the following:

Antiphon: Do not keep in mind, O Lord, our offenses or those of our parents, nor take vengeance on our sins. Our Father (the rest inaudibly until:)

P: And lead us not into temptation.

All: But deliver us from evil.

Psalm 53
After the psalm the priest continues:

P: Save your servant.

All: Who trusts in you, my God.

P: Let him (her) find in you, Lord, a fortified tower.

All: In the face of the enemy.

P: Let the enemy have no power over him (her).

Armor of God

All: And the son of iniquity be powerless to harm him (her). Lord, send him (her) aid from your holy place.

All: And watch over him (her) from Sion.

P: Lord, heed my prayer.

All: And let my cry be heard by you.

P: The Lord be with you.

All: May He also be with you.

Let us pray.
God, whose nature is ever merciful and forgiving, accept our prayer that this servant of yours, bound by the fetters of sin, may be pardoned by your loving kindness.

Holy Lord, almighty Father, everlasting God and Father of our Lord Jesus Christ, who once and for all consigned that fallen and apostate tyrant to the flames of hell, who sent your only-begotten Son into the world to crush that roaring lion; hasten to our call for help and snatch from ruination and from the clutches of the noonday devil this human being made in your image and likeness. Strike terror, Lord, into the beast now laying waste your vineyard. Fill your servants with courage to fight manfully against that reprobate dragon, lest he despise those who put their trust in you, and say with Pharaoh of old: "I know not God, nor will I set Israel free." Let your mighty hand cast him out of your servant, N., + so he may no longer hold captive this person whom it pleased you to make in your image, and to redeem through your Son; who lives and reigns with you, in the unity of the Holy Spirit, God, forever and ever.

All: Amen.

2. Then he commands the demon as follows:

I command you, unclean spirit, whoever you are, along with all your minions now attacking this servant of God, by the mysteries of the incarnation, passion, resurrection, and ascension of our Lord Jesus Christ, by the descent of the Holy Spirit, by the coming of our Lord for judgment, that you tell me by some sign your name, and the day and hour of your departure. I command you, moveover, to obey me to the letter, I who am a minister of God despite my unworthiness; nor shall you be emboldened to harm in any way this creature of God, or the bystanders, or any of their possessions.

3. Next he reads over the possessed person these selections from the Gospel, or at least one of them.

Armor of God

A Lesson from the holy Gospel according to St. John

John 1.1-14

As he says these opening words he signs himself and the possessed on the brow, lips, and breast.

A Lesson from the holy Gospel according to St. Mark

Mark 16.15-18

At that time Jesus said to His disciples: "Go into the whole world and preach the Gospel to all creation. He that believes and is baptized will be saved; he that does not believe will be condemned. And in the way of proofs of their claims, the following will accompany those who believe: in my name they will drive out demons; they will speak in new tongues; they will take up serpents in their hands, and if they drink something deadly, it will not hurt them; they will lay their hands on the sick, and these will recover."

A Lesson from the holy Gospel according to St. Luke

Luke 10.17-20

At that time the seventy-two returned in high spirits. "Master," they said, "even the demons are subject to us because we use your name!" "Yes," He said to them, "I was watching Satan fall like lightning that flashes from heaven. But mind: it is I that have given you the power to tread upon serpents and scorpions, and break the dominion of the enemy everywhere; nothing at all can injure you. Just the same, do not rejoice in the fact that the spirits are subject to you, but rejoice in the fact that your names are engraved in heaven."

A Lesson from the holy Gospel according to St. Luke

Luke 11.14-22

At that time Jesus was driving out a demon, and this particular demon was dumb. The demon was driven out, the dumb man spoke, and the crowds were enraptured. But some among the people remarked: "He is a tool of Beelzebul, and that is how he drives out demons!" Another group, intending to test Him, demanded of Him a proof of His claims, to be shown in the sky. He knew their inmost thoughts. "Any kingdom torn by civil strife," He said to them, "is laid in ruins; and house tumbles upon house. So, too, if Satan is in revolt against himself, how can his kingdom last, since you say that I drive out demons as a tool of Beelzebul. And furthermore: if I drive out demons as a tool of Beelzebul, whose tools are your pupils when they do the driving out? Therefore, judged by them, you must stand condemned. But, if, on the contrary, I drive out demons by the finger of God, then, evidently the kingdom of God has by this time made its way to you. As long as a mighty lord in full armor guards his premises, he is in peaceful possession of his property; but should one mightier than he attack and overcome him, he will strip him of his armor, on which he had relied, and distribute the spoils taken from him."

P: Lord, heed my prayer.

All: And let my cry be heard by you.

P: The Lord be with you.

All: May He also be with you.

Let us pray.

Almighty Lord, Word of God the Father, Jesus Christ, God and Lord of all creation; who gave to your holy apostles the power to tramp underfoot serpents and scorpions; who along with the other mandates to work miracles was pleased to grant them the authority to say: "Depart, you devils!" and by whose might Satan was made to fall from heaven like lightning; I humbly call on your holy name in fear and trembling, asking that you grant me, your unworthy servant, pardon for all my sins, steadfast faith, and the power--supported by your mighty arm--to confront with confidence and resolution this cruel demon. I ask this through you, Jesus Christ, our Lord and God, who are coming to judge both the living and the dead and the world by fire.

All: Amen.

4. Next he makes the sign of the cross over himself and the one possessed, places the end of the stole on the latter's neck, and, putting his right hand on the latter's head, he says the following in accents filled with confidence and faith:

P: See the cross of the Lord; begone, you hostile powers!

All: The stem of David, the lion of Juda's tribe has conquered.

P: Lord, heed my prayer.

All: And let my cry be heard by you.

P: The Lord be with you.

All: May He also be with you.

Let us pray.

God and Father of our Lord Jesus Christ, I appeal
to your holy name, humbly begging your kindness,
that you graciously grant me help against this and
every unclean spirit now tormenting this creature
of yours; through Christ our Lord.

All: Amen.

Exorcism

I cast you out, unclean spirit, along with every
satanic power of the enemy, every spectre from
hell, and all your fell companions; in the name of
our Lord Jesus + Christ Begone and stay far from
this creature of God. + For it is He who
commands you, He who flung you headlong from
the heights of heaven into the depths of hell. It is
He who commands you, He who once stilled the
sea and the wind and the storm. Hearken,
therefore, and tremble in fear, Satan, you enemy of
the faith, you foe of the human race, you begetter
of death, you robber of life, you corrupter of
justice, you root of all evil and vice? seducer of
men, betrayer of the nations, instigator of envy,
font of avarice, fomentor of discord, author of pain
and sorrow. Why, then, do you stand and resist,
knowing as you must that Christ the Lord brings
your plans to nothing? Fear Him, who in Isaac was

offered in sacrifice, in Joseph sold into bondage, slain as the paschal lamb, crucified as man, yet triumphed over the powers of hell. (The three signs of the cross which follow are traced on the brow of the possessed person). Begone, then, in the name of the Father, + and of the Son, + and of the Holy + Spirit. Give place to the Holy Spirit by this sign of the holy + cross of our Lord Jesus Christ, who lives and reigns with the Father and the Holy Spirit, God, forever and ever.

All: Amen.

P: Lord, heed my prayer.

All: And let my cry be heard by you.

P: The Lord be with you.

All: May He also be with you.

Let us pray.

God, Creator and defender of the human race, who made man in your own image, look down in pity on this your servant, N., now in the toils of the unclean spirit, now caught up in the fearsome threats of man's ancient enemy, sworn foe of our race, who befuddles and stupefies the human mind, throws it into terror, overwhelms it with fear and panic. Repel, O Lord, the devil's power, break

asunder his snares and traps, put the unholy
tempter to flight. By the sign + (on the brow) of
your name, let your servant be protected in mind
and body. (The three crosses which follow are
traced on the breast of the possessed person). Keep
watch over the inmost recesses of his (her) + heart;
rule over his (her) + emotions; strengthen his (her)
+ will. Let vanish from his (her) soul the temptings
of the mighty adversary. Graciously grant, O Lord,
as we call on your holy name, that the evil spirit,
who hitherto terrorized over us, may himself retreat
in terror and defeat, so that this servant of yours
may sincerely and steadfastly render you the service
which is your due; through Christ our Lord.

All: Amen.

Exorcism

I adjure you, ancient serpent, by the judge of the
living and the dead, by your Creator, by the Creator
of the whole universe, by Him who has the power
to consign you to hell, to depart forthwith in fear,
along with your savage minions, from this servant
of God, N., who seeks refuge in the fold of the
Church. I adjure you again, + (on the brow) not by
my weakness but by the might of the Holy Spirit, to
depart from this servant of God, N., whom
almighty God has made in His image. Yield,
therefore, yield not to my own person but to the
minister of Christ. For it is the power of Christ that

compels you, who brought you low by His cross. Tremble before that mighty arm that broke asunder the dark prison walls and led souls forth to light. May the trembling that afflicts this human frame, + (on the breast) the fear that afflicts this image (on the brow) of God, descend on you. Make no resistance nor delay in departing from this man, for it has pleased Christ to dwell in man. Do not think of despising my command because you know me to be a great sinner. It is God + Himself who commands you; the majestic Christ + who commands you. God the Father + commands you; God the Son + commands you; God the Holy + Spirit commands you. The mystery of the cross commands + you. The faith of the holy apostles Peter and Paul and of all the saints commands + you. The blood of the martyrs commands + you. The continence of the confessors commands + you. The devout prayers of all holy men and women command + you. The saving mysteries of our Christian faith command + you. Depart, then, transgressor. Depart, seducer, full of lies and cunning, foe of virtue, persecutor of the innocent. Give place, abominable creature, give way, you monster, give way to Christ, in whom you found none of your works. For He has already stripped you of your powers and laid waste your kingdom, bound you prisoner and plundered your weapons. He has cast you forth into the outer darkness, where everlasting ruin awaits you and your abettors. To what purpose do you insolently resist? To what purpose do you brazenly refuse? For you are guilty before almighty God, whose laws you have transgressed. You are guilty before His Son, our Lord Jesus Christ, whom you presumed to tempt, whom you dared to nail to the cross. You are guilty before the whole human race, to whom you proferred by your enticements the poisoned cup of death.

Therefore, I adjure you, profligate dragon, in the name of the spotless + Lamb, who has trodden down the asp and the basilisk, and overcome the lion and the dragon, to depart from this man (woman) + (on the brow), to depart from the Church of God + (signing the bystanders). Tremble and flee, as we call on the name of the Lord, before whom the denizens of hell cower, to whom the heavenly Virtues and Powers and Dominations are subject, whom the Cherubim and Seraphim praise with unending cries as they sing: Holy, holy, holy, Lord God of Sabaoth. The Word made flesh + commands you; the Virgin's Son + commands you; Jesus + of Nazareth commands you, who once, when you despised His disciples, forced you to flee in shameful defeat from a man; and when He had cast you out you did not even dare, except by His leave, to enter into a herd of swine. And now as I adjure you in His + name, begone from this man (woman) who is His creature. It is futile to resist His + will. It is hard for you to kick against the + goad. The longer you delay, the heavier your punishment shall be; for it is not men you are contemning, but rather Him who rules the living and the dead, who is coming to judge both the living and the dead and the world by fire.

All: Amen.

P: Lord, heed my prayer.

All: And let my cry be heard by you.

P: The Lord be with you.

All: May He also be with you.

Let us pray.

God of heaven and earth, God of the angels and archangels, God of the prophets and apostles, God of the martyrs and virgins, God who have power to bestow life after death and rest after toil; for there is no other God than you, nor can there be another true God beside you, the Creator of heaven and earth, who are truly a King, whose kingdom is without end; I humbly entreat your glorious majesty to deliver this servant of yours from the unclean spirits; through Christ our Lord.

All: Amen.

Exorcism

Therefore, I adjure you every unclean spirit, every spectre from hell, every satanic power, in the name of Jesus Christ of Nazareth, who was led into the desert after His baptism by John to vanquish you in your citadel, to cease your assaults against the creature whom He has formed from the slime of the earth for His own honor and glory; to quail before wretched man, seeing in him the image of almighty God, rather than his state of human frailty. Yield then to God, + who by His servant, Moses, cast you and your malice, in the person of Pharaoh and his army, into the depths of the sea. Yield to God, + who, by the singing of holy canticles on the part of David, His faithful servant, banished you from the heart of King Saul. Yield to God, + who condemned you in the person of Judas Iscariot, the traitor. For He now flails you with His divine scourges, + He in whose sight you and your legions once cried out: "What have we to do with you, Jesus, Son of the Most High God? Have you come to torture us before the time?" Now He is driving you back into the everlasting fire, He who at the end of time will say to the wicked: "Depart from me, you accursed, into the everlasting fire which has been prepared for the devil and his angels." For you, O evil one, and for your followers there will be worms that never die. An unquenchable fire stands ready for you and for your minions, you prince of accursed murderers, father of lechery, instigator of sacrileges, model of vileness, promoter of heresies, inventor of every obscenity.

Depart, then, + impious one, depart, + accursed one, depart with all your deceits, for God has willed that man should be His temple. Why do you still linger here? Give honor to God the Father + almighty, before whom every knee must bow. Give place to the Lord Jesus + Christ, who shed His most precious blood for man. Give place to the Holy + Spirit, who by His blessed apostle Peter openly struck you down in the person of Simon Magus; who cursed your lies in Annas and Saphira; who smote you in King Herod because he had not given honor to God; who by His apostle Paul afflicted you with the night of blindness in the magician Elyma, and by the mouth of the same apostle bade you to go out of Pythonissa, the soothsayer. Begone, + now! Begone, + seducer! Your place is in solitude; your abode is in the nest of serpents; get down and crawl with them. This matter brooks no delay; for see, the Lord, the ruler comes quickly, kindling fire before Him, and it will run on ahead of Him and encompass His enemies in flames. You might delude man, but God you cannot mock. It is He who casts you out, from whose sight nothing is hidden. It is He who repels you, to whose might all things are subject. It is He who expels you, He who has prepared everlasting hellfire for you and your angels, from whose mouth shall come a sharp sword, who is coming to judge both the living and the dead and the world by fire.

All: Amen.

5. All the above may be repeated as long as necessary, until the one possessed has been fully freed.

6. It will also help to say devoutly and often over the afflicted person the Our Father, Hail Mary, and the Creed, as well as any of the prayers given below.

7. The Canticle of our Lady, with the doxology; the Canticle of Zachary, with the doxology.

Athanasian Creed

P: Whoever wills to be saved * must before all else hold fast to the Catholic faith.

All: Unless one keeps this faith whole and untarnished, * without doubt he will perish forever.

P: Now this is the Catholic faith: * that we worship one God in Trinity, and Trinity in unity;

All: Neither confusing the Persons one with the other, * nor making a distinction in their nature.

Armor of God

P: For the Father is a distinct Person; and so is the Son, * and so is the Holy Spirit.

All: Yet the Father, Son, and Holy Spirit possess one Godhead, * co-equal glory, co-eternal majesty.

P: As the Father is, so is the Son, * so also is the Holy Spirit.
All: The Father is uncreated, the Son is uncreated, * the Holy Spirit is uncreated.

P: The Father is infinite, the Son is infinite, * the Holy Spirit is infinite.

All: The Father is eternal, the Son is eternal, * the Holy Spirit is eternal.

P: Yet they are not three eternals, * but one eternal God.

All: Even as they are not three uncreated, or three infinites, * but one uncreated and one infinite God.

P: So likewise the Father is almighty, the Son is almighty, * the Holy Spirit is almighty.

All: Yet they are not three almighties, * but they are the one Almighty.

P: Thus the Father is God, the Son is God, * the Holy Spirit is God.

Armor of God

All: Yet they are not three gods, * but one God.

P: Thus the Father is Lord, the Son is Lord, * the Holy Spirit is Lord.

All: Yet there are not three lords, * but one Lord.

P: For just as Christian truth compels us to profess that each Person is individually God and Lord, * so does the Catholic religion forbid us to hold that there are three gods or lords.

All: The Father was not made by any power; * He was neither created nor begotten.

P: The Son is from the Father alone, * neither created nor made, but begotten.

All: The Holy Spirit is from the Father and the Son, * neither made nor created nor begotten, but He proceeds.

P: So there is one Father, not three; one Son, not three; * one Holy Spirit, not three.

All: And in this Trinity one Person is not earlier or later, nor is one greater or less; * but all three Persons are co-eternal and co-equal.

P: In every way, then, as already affirmed, * unity in Trinity and Trinity in unity is to be worshipped.

Armor of God

All: Whoever, then, wills to be saved * must assent to this doctrine of the Blessed Trinity.

P: But it is necessary for everlasting salvation * that one also firmly believe in the incarnation of our Lord Jesus Christ.

All: True faith, then, requires us to believe and profess * that our Lord Jesus Christ, the Son of God, is both God and man.

P: He is God, begotten of the substance of the Father from eternity; * He is man, born in time of the substance of His Mother.

All: He is perfect God, and perfect man * subsisting in a rational soul and a human body.

P: He is equal to the Father in His divine nature, * but less than the Father in His human nature as such.

All: And though He is God and man, * yet He is the one Christ, not two;

P: One, however, not by any change of divinity into flesh, * but by the act of God assuming a human nature. All: He is one only, not by a mixture of substance, * but by the oneness of His Person.

Armor of God

P: For, somewhat as the rational soul and the body compose one man, * so Christ is one Person who is both God and man;

All: Who suffered for our salvation, who descended into hell, * who rose again the third day from the dead;

P: Who ascended into heaven, and sits at the right hand of God the Father almighty, * from there He shall come to judge both the living and the dead.

All: At His coming all men shall rise again in their bodies, * and shall give an account of their works.

P: And those who have done good shall enter into everlasting life, * but those who have done evil into ever lasting fire.

All: All this is Catholic faith, * and unless one believes it truly and firmly one cannot be saved.

P: Glory be to the Father

All: As it was in the beginning.

{Here follow a large number of psalms which may be used at the exorcist's discretion but are not a necessary part of the rite. Some of them occur in other parts of the Ritual and are so indicated; the others may be taken from the Psalter. Psalm 90;

psalm 67; psalm 69; psalm 53; psalm 117; psalm 34; psalm 30; psalm 21, psalm 3; psalm 10; psalm 12.}

Prayer Following Deliverance

Almighty God, we beg you to keep the evil spirit from further molesting this servant of yours, and to keep him far away, never to return. At your command, O Lord, may the goodness and peace of our Lord Jesus Christ, our Redeemer, take possession of this man (woman). May we no longer fear any evil since the Lord is with us; who lives and reigns with you, in the unity of the Holy Spirit, God, forever and ever.

All: Amen.

Chapter III: Exorcism Of Satan And The Fallen Angels

{Whereas the preceding rite of exorcism is designated for a particular person, the present one is for general use--to combat the power of the evil spirits over a community or locality.}

The following exorcism can be used by bishops, as well as by priests who have this authorization from their Ordinary.

In the name of the Father, and of the Son, and of the Holy Spirit. Amen.

Armor of God

Prayer to St. Michael the Archangel

St. Michael the Archangel, illustrious leader of the heavenly army, defend us in the battle against principalities and powers, against the rulers of the world of darkness and the spirit of wickedness in high places. Come to the rescue of mankind, whom God has made in His own image and likeness, and purchased from Satan's tyranny at so great a price. Holy Church venerates you as her patron and guardian. The Lord has entrusted to you the task of leading the souls of the redeemed to heavenly blessedness. Entreat the Lord of peace to cast Satan down under our feet, so as to keep him from further holding man captive and doing harm to the Church. Carry our prayers up to God's throne, that the mercy of the Lord may quickly come and lay hold of the beast, the serpent of old, Satan and his demons, casting him in chains into the abyss, so that he can no longer seduce the nations.

Exorcism

In the name of Jesus Christ, our Lord and God, by the intercession of Mary, spotless Virgin and Mother of God, of St. Michael the Archangel, of the blessed apostles Peter and Paul, and of all the saints, and by the authority residing in our holy ministry, we steadfastly proceed to combat the onslaught of the wily enemy.

Armor of God

Psalm 67

P: God arises; His enemies are scattered, * and those who hate Him flee before Him.

All: As smoke is driven away, so are they driven; * as wax melts before the fire, so the wicked perish before God.

P: See the cross of the Lord; begone, you hostile powers!

All: The stem of David, the lion of Juda's tribe has conquered.

P: May your mercy, Lord, remain with us always.

All: For we put our whole trust in you.

We cast you out, every unclean spirit, every satanic power, every onslaught of the infernal adversary, every legion, every diabolical group and sect, in the name and by the power of our Lord Jesus + Christ. We command you, begone and fly far from the Church of God, from the souls made by God in His image and redeemed by the precious blood of the divine Lamb. + No longer dare, cunning serpent, to deceive the human race, to persecute

God's Church, to strike God's elect and to sift them as wheat. + For the Most High God commands you, + He to whom you once proudly presumed yourself equal; He who wills all men to be saved and come to the knowledge of truth. God the Father + commands you. God the Son + commands you. God the Holy + Spirit commands you. Christ, the eternal Word of God made flesh, commands you, who humbled Himself, becoming obedient even unto death, to save our race from the perdition wrought by your envy; who founded His Church upon a firm rock, declaring that the gates of hell should never prevail against her, and that He would remain with her all days, even to the end of the world. The sacred mystery of the cross + commands you, along with the power of all mysteries of Christian faith. + The exalted Virgin Mary, Mother of God, + commands you, who in her lowliness crushed your proud head from the first moment of her Immaculate Conception. The faith of the holy apostles Peter and Paul and the other apostles + commands you. The blood of martyrs and the devout prayers of all holy men and women command + you.

Therefore, accursed dragon and every diabolical legion, we adjure you by the living + God, by the true + God, by the holy + God, by God, who so loved the world that He gave His only-begotten Son, that whoever believes in Him might not perish but have everlasting life; to cease deluding human creatures and filling them with the poison of everlasting damnation; to desist from harming the Church and hampering her freedom. Begone, Satan, father and master of lies, enemy of man's welfare. Give place to Christ, in whom you found none of your works. Give way to the one, holy, catholic, and apostolic Church, which Christ Himself purchased with His blood. Bow down before God's mighty hand, tremble and flee as we call on the holy and awesome name of Jesus, before whom the denizens of hell cower, to whom the heavenly Virtues and Powers and Dominations are subject, whom the Cherubim and Seraphim praise with unending cries as they sing: Holy, holy, holy, Lord God of Sabaoth.

P: Lord, heed my prayer.

All: And let my cry be heard by you.

P: The Lord be with you.

All: May He also be with you.

Let us pray.

God of heaven and earth, God of the angels and archangels, God of the patriarchs and prophets, God of the apostles and martyrs, God of the confessors and virgin God who have power to bestow life after death and rest after toil; for there is no other God than you, nor can there be another true God beside you, the Creator of all things visible and invisible, whose kingdom is without end; we humbly entreat your glorious majesty to deliver us by your might from every influence of the accursed spirits, from their every evil snare and deception, and to keep us from all harm; through Christ our Lord.

All: Amen.

P: From the snares of the devil.

All: Lord, deliver us.

P: That you help your Church to serve you in security and freedom.

All: We beg you to hear us.

P: That you humble the enemies of holy Church.

All: We beg you to hear us.

The surroundings are sprinkled with holy water.

Armor of God

1999 Rite of Exorcism for the Catholic Church

P: Lord, have mercy.
All: Lord, have mercy.

P: Christ, have mercy.
All: Christ, have mercy.

P: Lord, have mercy.
All: Lord, have mercy.

P: Christ, hear us.
All: Christ, graciously hear us.
P: God, the Father in heaven.
All: Have mercy on us.

P: God, the Son, Redeemer of the world.
All: Have mercy on us.

P: God, the Holy Spirit.
All: Have mercy on us.

P: Holy Trinity, one God.
All: Have mercy on us.

Holy Mary, pray for us,*
* After each invocation: "Pray for us."

Holy Mother of God,
Holy Virgin of virgins,
St. Michael,
St. Gabriel,
St. Raphael,
All holy angels and archangels,
All holy orders of blessed spirits,
St. John the Baptist,
St. Joseph,
All holy patriarchs and prophets,
St. Peter,
St. Paul,
St. Andrew,
St. James,
St. John,
St. Thomas,
St. James,
St. Philip,
St. Bartholomew,
St. Matthew,
St. Simon,
St. Thaddeus,
St. Matthias,
St. Barnabas,
St. Luke,

St. Mark,
All holy apostles and evangelists,
All holy disciples of the Lord,
All holy Innocents,
St. Stephen,
St. Lawrence,
St. Vincent,
SS. Fabian and Sebastian,
SS. John and Paul,
SS. Cosmas and Damian,
SS. Gervase and Protase,
All holy martyrs,
St. Sylvester,
St. Gregory,
St. Ambrose,
St. Augustine,
St. Jerome,
St. Martin,
St. Nicholas,
All holy bishops and confessors,
All holy doctors,
St. Anthony,
St. Benedict,
St. Bernard,
St. Dominic,
St. Francis,
All holy priests and levites,
All holy monks and hermits,
St. Mary Magdalene,
St. Agatha,
St. Lucy,

Armor of God

St. Agnes,
St. Cecilia,
St. Catherine,
St. Anastasia,
All holy virgins and widows,

P: All holy saints of God,
All: Intercede for us.

P: Be merciful,
All: Spare us, 0 Lord.

P: Be merciful,
All: Graciously hear us, 0 Lord.

From all evil, deliver us, 0 Lord.*
* After each invocation: "Deliver us, 0 Lord."

From all sin,
From your wrath,
From sudden and unprovided death,
From the snares of the devil,
From anger, hatred, and all ill will,
From all lewdness,
From lightning and tempest,
From the scourge of earthquakes,
From plague, famine, and war,
From everlasting death,
By the mystery of your holy incarnation,
By your coming,
By your birth,

135

Armor of God

By your baptism and holy fasting,
By your cross and passion,
By your death and burial,
By your holy resurrection,
By your wondrous ascension,
By the coming of the Holy,
Spirit, the Advocate,
On the day of judgment,

P: We sinners,
All: We beg you to hear us.*
* After each invocation: "We beg you to hear us."

That you spare us,
That you pardon us,
That you bring us to true penance,
That you govern and preserve your holy Church,
That you preserve our Holy Father and all ranks in
the Church in holy religion,
That you humble the enemies of holy Church,
That you give peace and true concord to all
Christian rulers. That you give peace and unity to
the whole Christian world, That you restore to the
unity of the Church all who have strayed from the
truth, and lead all unbelievers to the light of the
Gospel, That you confirm and preserve us in your
holy service, That you lift up our minds to heavenly
desires, That you grant everlasting blessings to all
our benefactors, That you deliver our souls and the
souls of our brethren, relatives, and benefactors
from everlasting damnation, That you give and

preserve the fruits of the earth, That you grant eternal rest to all the faithful departed, That you graciously hear us, Son of God,

At the end of the litany he (the priest) adds the following:

P: Antiphon: Do not keep in mind, 0 Lord, our offenses or those of our parents, nor take vengeance on our sins.

P: Our Father
who art in heaven,
hallowed be thy name;
thy kingdom come;
thy will be done on earth as it is in heaven.
Give us this day our daily bread;
and forgive us our trespasses
as we forgive those who trespass against us;
and lead us not into temptation,

All: But deliver us from evil.

Psalm 53

P: God, by your name save me, and by your might defend my cause.
All: God, hear my prayer; hearken to the words of my mouth.

P: For haughty men have risen up against me,

and fierce men seek my life; they set not God before their eyes.

All: See, God is my helper; the Lord sustains my life.

P: Turn back the evil upon my foes; in your faithfulness destroy them.
All: Freely will I offer you sacrifice; I will praise your name, Lord, for its goodness,

P: Because from all distress you have rescued me, and my eyes look down upon my enemies.
All: Glory be to the Father.

P: As it was in the beginning.
After the psalm the priest continues:

P: Save your servant.
All: Who trusts in you, my God.

P: Let him (her) find in you, Lord, a fortified tower.
All: In the face of the enemy.

P: Let the enemy have no power over him (her).
All: And the son of iniquity be powerless to harm him (her).

P: Lord, send him (her) aid from your holy place.
All: And watch over him (her) from Sion.

Armor of God

P: Lord, heed my prayer.
All: And let my cry be heard by you.

P: The Lord be with you.
All: May He also be with you.

Let us pray.

God, whose nature is ever merciful and forgiving, accept our prayer that this   servant of yours, bound by the fetters of sin, may be pardoned by your loving   kindness. Holy Lord, almighty Father, everlasting God and Father of our Lord Jesus   Christ, who once and for all consigned that fallen and apostate tyrant to the flames of hell, who sent your only-begotten Son into the world to crush that   roaring lion; hasten to our call for help and snatch from ruination and from the clutches of the noonday devil this human being made in your image and likeness. Strike terror, Lord, into the beast now laying waste your vineyard.
Fill your servants with courage to fight manfully against that reprobate dragon, lest he despise those who put their trust in you, and say with Pharaoh of old: "I know not God, nor will I set Israel free." Let your mighty hand cast him out of your servant, (The name of the person), so he may no longer hold captive this person whom it pleased you to make in your image, and to redeem through your Son; who lives and reigns with you, in the unity of the Holy Spirit, God, forever and ever.

All: Amen.

Then he commands the demon as follows:
I command you, unclean spirit, whoever you are,
along with all your minions now attacking this
servant of God, by the mysteries of the incarnation,
passion, resurrection, and ascension of our Lord
Jesus Christ, by the descent of the Holy Spirit, by
the coming of our Lord for judgment, that you tell
me by some sign your name, and the day and hour
of your departure. I command you, moreover, to
obey me to the letter, I who am a minister of God
despite my unworthiness; nor shall you be
emboldened to harm in any way this creature of
God, or the bystanders, or any of their ossessions.
The priest lays his hand on the head of the sick
person, saying: They shall lay their hands upon the
sick and all will be well with them. May Jesus, Son
of Mary, Lord and Savior of the world, through the
merits and intercession of His holy apostles Peter
and Paul and all His saints, show you favor and
mercy.

All: Amen.

Next he reads over the possessed person these
selections from the Gospel, or at least one of them.

P: The Lord be with you.
All: May He also be with you.

P: The beginning of the holy Gospel according to St. John.

All: Glory be to you, 0 Lord.

A Lesson from the holy Gospel according to St. John (John 1:1-14)

As he says these opening words he signs himself and the possessed on the brow, lips, and breast.

When time began, the Word was there, and the Word was face to face with God,   and the Word was God. This Word, when time began, was face to face with God.   All things came into being through Him, and without Him there came to be not one thing that has come to be. In Him was life, and the life was the light of men. The light shines in the darkness, and the darkness did not lay hold of it. There came upon the scene a man, a messenger from God, whose name was John. This man came to give testimony to testify in behalf of the light that all might believe through him. He was not himself the light; he only was to testify in behalf of the light. Meanwhile the true light, which illumines every man, was making its entrance into the world. He was in the world, and the world came to be through Him, and the world did not acknowledge Him. He came into His home, and His own people did not welcome Him. But to as many as welcomed Him He gave the power to become children of

141

God those who believe in His name; who were born not of blood, or of carnal desire, or of man's will; no, they were born of God. (Genuflect here.) And the Word became man and lived among us; and we have looked upon His glory such a glory as befits the Father's only-begotten Son full of grace and truth!

All: Thanks be to God.

Lastly he blesses the sick person, saying:

May the blessing of almighty God, Father, Son, and Holy Spirit, come upon you and remain with you forever.

All: Amen.

Then he sprinkles the person with holy water.

A Lesson from the holy Gospel according to St. Mark (Mark 16:15-18)

At that time Jesus said to His disciples: "Go into the whole world and preach the Gospel to all creation. He that believes and is baptized will be saved; he that does not believe will be condemned. And in the way of proofs of their claims, the following will accompany those who believe: in my name they will drive out demons; they will speak in new tongues; they will take up serpents in their hands, and if they drink something deadly, it will not hurt them; they will lay their hands on the sick, and these will recover."

A Lesson from the holy Gospel according to St. Luke (Luke 10:17-20)

At that time the seventy-two returned in high spirits. "Master," they said, "even the demons are subject to us because we use your name!" "Yes," He said to them, "I was watching Satan fall like lightning that flashes from heaven. But mind: it is I that have given you the power to tread upon serpents and scorpions, and break the dominion of the enemy everywhere; nothing at all can injure you. Just the same, do not rejoice in the fact that the spirits are subject to you, but rejoice in the fact that your names are engraved in heaven."

A Lesson from the holy Gospel according to St. Luke (Luke 11:14-22)

At that time Jesus was driving out a demon, and this particular demon was dumb. The demon was driven out, the dumb man spoke, and the crowds were enraptured. But some among the people remarked: "He is a tool of Beelzebul, and that is how he drives out demons!" Another group, intending to test Him, demanded of Him a proof of His claims, to be shown in the sky. He knew their inmost thoughts. "Any kingdom torn by civil strife," He said to them, "is laid in ruins; and house tumbles upon house. So, too, if Satan is in revolt against himself, how can his kingdom last, since you say that I drive out demons as a tool of Beelzebul. And furthermore: if I drive out demons as a tool of Beelzebul, whose tools are your pupils when they do the driving out? Therefore, judged by them, you must stand condemned. But, if, on the contrary, I drive out demons by the finger of God, then, evidently the kingdom of God has by this time made its way to you. As long as a mighty lord in full armor guards his premises, he is in peaceful possession of his property; but should one mightier than he attack and overcome him, he will strip him of his armor, on which he had relied, and distribute the spoils taken from him."

P: Lord, heed my prayer.
All: And let my cry be heard by you.

P: The Lord be with you.
All: May He also be with you.

Let us pray.

Almighty Lord, Word of God the Father, Jesus Christ, God and Lord of all creation; who gave to your holy apostles the power to tramp underfoot serpents and scorpions; who along with the other mandates to work miracles was pleased to grant them the authority to say: "Depart, you devils!" and by whose might Satan was made to fall from heaven like lightning; I humbly call on your holy name in fear and trembling, asking that you grant me, your unworthy servant, pardon for all my sins, steadfast faith, and the power - supported by your mighty arm - to confront with confidence and resolution this cruel demon. I ask this through you, Jesus Christ, our Lord and God, who are coming to judge both the living and the dead and the world by fire.

All: Amen.

Next he makes the sign of the cross over himself and the one possessed, places the end of the stole on the latter's neck, and, putting his right hand on the latter's head, he says the following in accents filled with confidence and faith:

P: See the cross of the Lord;   begone, you hostile powers!
All: The stem of David, the lion of Juda's tribe has conquered.

P: Lord, heed my prayer.
All: And let my cry be heard by you.

P: The Lord be with you.
All: May He also be with you.

Let us pray.

God and Father of our Lord Jesus Christ, I appeal to your holy name, humbly begging your kindness, that you graciously grant me help against this and every unclean spirit now tormenting this creature of yours; through Christ our Lord.

All: Amen.

Exorcism

I cast you out, unclean spirit, along with every Satanic power of the enemy, every spectre from hell, and all your fell companions; in the name of our Lord Jesus +Christ. Begone and stay far from this creature of God.+ For it is He who commands you, He who flung you headlong from the heights of heaven into the depths of hell. It is He who commands you, He who once stilled the sea and the wind and the storm. Hearken, therefore, and tremble in fear, Satan, you enemy of the faith, you foe of the human race, you begetter of death, you robber of life, you corrupter of justice, you root of all evil and vice;   seducer of men, betrayer of the nations, instigator of envy, font of avarice, fomentor of discord, author of pain and sorrow. Why, then, do you stand and resist, knowing as you must that Christ the Lord brings your plans to nothing? Fear Him, who in Isaac was offered in sacrifice, in Joseph sold into bondage, slain as the paschal lamb, crucified as man, yet triumphed over the powers of hell. (The three signs of the cross

146

which follow are traced on the brow of the possessed person). Begone, then, in the name of the Father, + and of the Son, + and of the Holy + Spirit. Give place to the Holy Spirit by this sign of the holy + cross of our Lord Jesus Christ, who lives and reigns with the Father and the Holy Spirit, God, forever and ever.

All: Amen.

P: Lord, heed my prayer.

All: And let my cry be heard by you.

P: The Lord be with you.

All: May He also be with you.

Let us pray.

God, Creator and defender of the human race, who made man in your own image, look down in pity on this your servant, N., now in the toils of the unclean spirit, now caught up in the fearsome threats of man's ancient enemy, sworn foe of our race, who befuddles and stupefies the human mind, throws it into terror, overwhelms it with fear and panic. Repel, 0 Lord, the devil's power, break asunder his snares and traps, put the unholy tempter to flight. By the sign + (on the brow) of your name, let your servant be protected in mind and body. (The three crosses which follow are traced on the breast of the possessed person). Keep watch over the inmost recesses of his (her) + heart; rule over his (her) + emotions; strengthen his (her) + will. Let vanish from his (her) soul the temptings of the mighty adversary. Graciously grant, 0 Lord, as we call on your holy name, that the evil spirit, who hitherto terrorized over us, may himself retreat in terror and defeat, so that this servant of yours may sincerely and steadfastly render you the service which is your due; through Christ our Lord.

All: Amen.

Exorcism

I adjure you, ancient serpent, by the judge of the living and the dead, by your Creator, by the Creator of the whole universe, by Him who has the power to consign you to hell, to depart forthwith in fear, along with your savage minions, from this servant of God, N., who seeks refuge in the fold of the Church. I adjure you again, + (on the brow) not by my weakness but by the might of the Holy Spirit, to depart from this servant of God, N. , whom almighty God has made in His image. Yield, therefore, yield not to my own person but to the minister of Christ. For it is the power of Christ that compels you, who brought you low by His cross. Tremble before that mighty arm that broke asunder the dark prison walls and led souls forth to light.

May the trembling that afflicts this human frame, + on the breast) the fear that afflicts this image + (on the brow) of God, descend on you. Make no resistance nor delay in departing from this man, for it has pleased Christ to dwell in man. Do not think of despising my command because you know me to be a great sinner. It is God + Himself who commands you; the majestic Christ + who commands you. God the Father + commands you; God the Son + commands you; God the Holy + Spirit commands you. The mystery of the cross commands +you. The faith of the holy apostles Peter and Paul and of all the saints commands + you. The blood of the martyrs commands + you. The continence of the confessors commands + you. The devout prayers of all holy men and women command + you. The saving mysteries of our Christian faith command + you. Depart, then, transgressor. Depart, seducer, full of lies and cunning, foe of virtue, persecutor of the innocent. Give place, abominable creature, give way, you monster, give way to Christ, in whom you found none of your works. For He has already stripped you of your powers and laid waste your kingdom, bound you prisoner and plundered your weapons. He has cast you forth into the outer darkness, where everlasting ruin awaits you and your abettors. To what purpose do you insolently resist? To what purpose do you brazenly refuse? For you are guilty before almighty God, whose laws you have transgressed. You are guilty before His Son, our Lord Jesus Christ, whom you presumed to tempt, whom you dared to nail to the cross. You are guilty before the whole human race, to whom you proferred by your enticements the poisoned cup of death. Therefore, I adjure you, profligate dragon, in the name of the spotless + Lamb, who has trodden down the asp and the basilisk, and overcome the lion and the dragon, to depart from this man (woman) + (on the brow), to depart from the Church of God + (signing the bystanders). Tremble and flee, as we call on the name of the Lord, before whom the denizens of hell cower, to whom the heavenly Virtues and Powers and Dominations are subject, whom the Cherubim and Seraphim praise with unending cries as they sing: Holy, holy, holy, Lord God of Sabaoth. The Word made flesh + commands you; the Virgin's Son + commands you; Jesus + of Nazareth commands you, who once, when you despised His disciples, forced you to flee in shameful defeat from a man; and when He had cast you out you did not even dare, except by His leave, to enter into a herd of swine. And now as I adjure you in His + name, begone from this man (woman) who is His creature. It is futile to resist His + will. It is hard for you to kick against the + goad. The longer you delay, the heavier your punishment shall be; for it is not men you are condemning, but rather Him who rules the living and the dead, who is coming to judge both the living and the dead and the world by fire.

All: Amen.

P: Lord, heed my prayer.

All: And let my cry be heard by you.

P: The Lord be with you.

All: May He also be with you.

Let us pray.

God of heaven and earth, God of the angels and archangels, God of the prophets and apostles, God of the martyrs and virgins, God who have power to bestow life after death and rest after toil; for there is no other God than you, nor can there be another true God beside you, the Creator of heaven and earth, who are truly a King, whose kingdom is without end; I humbly entreat your glorious majesty to deliver this servant of yours from the unclean spirits; through Christ our Lord.

All: Amen.

Exorcism

Therefore, I adjure you every unclean spirit, every spectre from hell, every satanic power, in the name of Jesus + Christ of Nazareth, who was led into the desert after His baptism by John to vanquish you in your citadel, to cease your assaults against the creature whom He has, formed from the slime of the earth for His own honor and glory; to quail before wretched man, seeing in him the image of almighty God, rather than his state of human frailty. Yield then to God, + who by His servant, Moses, cast you and your malice, in the person of Pharaoh and his army, into the depths of the sea. Yield to God, + who, by the singing of holy canticles on the part of David, His faithful servant, banished you from the heart of King Saul. Yield to God, + who condemned you in the person of Judas Iscariot, the traitor. For He now flails you with His divine scourges, + He in whose sight you and your legions once cried out: "What have we to do with you, Jesus, Son of the Most High God? Have you come to torture us before the time?" Now He is driving you back into the everlasting fire, He who at the end of time will say to the wicked: "Depart from me, you accursed, into the everlasting fire which has been prepared for the devil and his angels." For you, 0 evil one, and for your followers there will be worms that never die. An unquenchable fire stands ready for you and for your minions, you prince of accursed murderers, father of lechery, instigator of sacrileges, model of vileness, promoter of heresies, inventor of every obscenity. Depart, then, + impious one, depart, + accursed one, depart with all your deceits, for God has willed that man should be His temple. Why do you still linger here? Give honor to God the Father + almighty, before whom every knee must bow. Give place to the Lord Jesus + Christ, who shed His most precious blood for man. Give place to the Holy + Spirit, who by His blessed apostle Peter openly struck you down in the person of Simon Magus; who cursed your lies in Annas and Saphira; who smote you in King Herod because he had not given honor to God; who by His apostle Paul afflicted you with the night of blindness in the magician Elyma, and by the mouth of the same apostle bade you to go out of Pythonissa, the soothsayer. Begone, + now! Begone, + seducer! Your place is in solitude; your abode is in the nest of serpents; get down and crawl with them. This matter brooks no delay; for see, the Lord, the ruler comes quickly, kindling fire before Him, and it will run on ahead of Him and encompass His enemies in flames. You might delude man, but God you cannot mock. It is He who casts you out, from whose sight nothing is hidden. It is He who repels you, to whose might all things are subject. It is He who expels you, He who has prepared everlasting hellfire for you and your angels, from whose mouth shall come a sharp sword, who is coming to judge both the living and the dead and the world by fire.

All: Amen.

All the above may be repeated as long as necessary, until the one possessed has been fully freed. It will also help to say devoutly and often over the afflicted person the Our Father, Hail Mary, and the Creed, as well as any of the prayers given below. The Canticle of our Lady, with the doxology; the Canticle of Zachary, with the doxology.

P: Antiphon: Magi from the East came to Bethlehem to adore the Lord; and opening their treasure chests they presented Him with precious gifts: Gold for the great King, incense for the true God, and myrrh in symbol of His burial. Alleluia.

Canticle of Our Lady
(The Magnificat)
(Luke 1:46-55)

P: "My soul extols the Lord;

All: And my spirit leaps for joy in God my Savior.

P: How graciously He looked upon His lowly maid! Oh, see, from this hour onward age after age will call me blessed!

All: How sublime is what He has done for me, the Mighty One, whose name is `Holy'!

P: From age to age He visits those who worship Him in reverence.

All: His arm achieves the mastery: He routs the haughty and proud of heart.

P: He puts down princes from their thrones, and exalts the lowly;

All: He fills the hungry with blessings, and sends away the rich with empty hands.

P: He has taken by the hand His servant Israel, and mercifully kept His faith,

All: As He had promised our fathers with Abraham and his posterity forever and evermore."

P: Glory be to the Father.

All: As it was in the beginning.

Antiphon: Magi from the East came to Bethlehem to adore the Lord; and opening their treasure chests they presented Him with precious gifts: Gold for the great King, incense for the true God, and myrrh in symbol of His burial. Alleluia.

Meanwhile the home is sprinkled with holy water and incensed. Then the priest says:

P: Our Father
who art in Heaven,
Hallowed be Thy Name;

Armor of God

Thy Kingdom come;
Thy will be done on earth
As it is in Heaven.
Give us this day our daily bread;
and forgive us our trespasses
as we forgive those who trespass against us,
and lead us not into temptation.

All: But deliver us from evil.

P: Many shall come from Saba.

All: Bearing gold and incense.

P: Lord, heed my prayer.

All: And let my cry be heard by you.

P: The Lord be with you.
All: May he also be with you.

Let us pray.
God, who on this day revealed your only-begotten
Son to all nations by the guidance of a star, grant
that we who now know you by faith may finally
behold you in your heavenly majesty; through
Christ our Lord.

All: Amen.

Armor of God

Responsory: Be enlightened and shine forth, 0 Jerusalem, for your light is come; and upon you is risen the glory of the Lord Jesus Christ born of the Virgin Mary.

P: Nations shall walk in your light, and kings in the splendor of your birth. All: And the glory of the Lord is risen upon you.

Let us pray.
Lord God almighty, bless +this home, and under its shelter let there be health, chastity, self-conquest, humility, goodness, mildness, obedience to your commandments, and thanksgiving to God the Father, Son, and Holy Spirit. May your blessing remain always in this home and on those who live here; through Christ our Lord.

All: Amen.

P: Antiphon for Canticle of Zachary:

Today the Church is espoused to her heavenly bridegroom, for Christ washes her sins in the Jordan; the Magi hasten with gifts to the regal nuptials; and the guests are gladdened with water made wine, alleluia.

Canticle of Zachary(Luke 1:68-79

P: "Blessed be the Lord, the God of Israel!

Armor of God

He has visited His people and brought about its redemption.

All: He has raised for us a stronghold of salvation in the house of David His servant,

P: And redeemed the promise He had made through the mouth of His holy prophets of old

All: To grant salvation from our foes and from the hand of all that hate us;

P: To deal in mercy with our fathers and be mindful of His holy covenant,

All: Of the oath he had sworn to our father Abraham, that He would enable us

P: Rescued from the clutches of our foes to worship Him without fear,

All: In holiness and observance of the Law, in His presence, all our days.

P: And you, my little one, will be hailed `Prophet of the Most High'; for the Lord's precursor you will be to prepare His ways;

All: You are to impart to His people knowledge of salvation through forgiveness of their sins.

P: Thanks be to the merciful heart of our God! a dawning Light from on high will visit us

All: To shine upon those who sit in darkness and in the shadowland of death, and guide our feet into the path of peace."

P: Glory be to the Father.

All: As it was in the beginning.

Antiphon:

Today the Church is espoused to her heavenly bridegroom, for Christ washes her sins in the Jordan; the Magi hasten with gifts to the regal nuptials; and the guests are gladdened with water made wine, alleluia.

Then the celebrant sings:

P: The Lord be with you.

All: May He also be with you.

Let us pray.
God, who on this day revealed your only-begotten Son to all nations by the guidance of a star, grant that we who now know you by faith may finally behold you in your heavenly majesty; through Christ our Lord.

All: Amen.

Athanasian Creed

P: Whoever wills to be saved must before all else hold fast to the Catholic faith.

All: Unless one keeps this faith whole and untarnished, without doubt he will perish forever.

P: Now this is the Catholic faith: that we worship one God in Trinity, and Trinity in unity;

All: Neither confusing the Persons one with the other, nor making a distinction in their nature.

P: For the Father is a distinct Person; and so is the Son; and so is the Holy Spirit.

All: Yet the Father, Son, and Holy Spirit possess one Godhead, co-equal glory, co-eternal majesty.

P: As the Father is, so is the Son, so also is the Holy Spirit.

All: The Father is uncreated, the Son is uncreated, the Holy Spirit is uncreated.

P: The Father is infinite, the Son is infinite, the Holy Spirit is infinite.

Armor of God

All: The Father is eternal, the Son is eternal, the Holy Spirit is eternal.

P: Yet they are not three eternals, but one eternal God.

All: Even as they are not three uncreated, or three infinites, but one uncreated and one infinite God.

P: So likewise the Father is almighty, the Son is almighty, the Holy Spirit is almighty.

All: Yet they are not three almighties, but they are the one Almighty.

P: Thus the Father is God, the Son is God, the Holy Spirit is God.

All: Yet they are not three gods, but one God.

P: Thus the Father is Lord, the Son is Lord, the Holy Spirit is Lord.

All: Yet there are not three lords, but one Lord.

P: For just as Christian truth compels us to profess that each Person is individually God and Lord, so does the Catholic religion forbid us to hold that there are three gods or lords.

All: The Father was not made by any power;

Armor of God

He was neither created nor begotten.

P: The Son is from the Father alone, neither created nor made, but begotten.

All: The Holy Spirit is from the Father and the Son, neither made nor created nor begotten, but He proceeds.

P: So there is one Father, not three; one Son, not three; one Holy Spirit, not three.

All: And in this Trinity one Person is not earlier or later, nor is one greater or less; but all three Persons are co-eternal and co-equal.

P: In every way, then, as already affirmed, unity in Trinity and Trinity in unity is to be worshiped.

All: Whoever, then, wills to be saved must assent to this doctrine of the Blessed Trinity.

P: But it is necessary for everlasting salvation that one also firmly believe in the incarnation of our Lord Jesus Christ.

All: True faith, then, requires us to believe and profess that our Lord Jesus Christ, the Son of God, is both God and man.

P: He is God, begotten of the substance of the Father from eternity; He is man, born in time of the substance of His Mother.

All: He is perfect God, and perfect man subsisting in a rational soul and a human body.

P: He is equal to the Father in His divine nature, but less than the Father in His human nature as such.

All: And though He is God and man, yet He is the one Christ, not two;

P: One, however, not by any change of divinity into flesh, but by the act of God assuming a human nature.

All: He is one only, not by a mixture of substance, but by the oneness of His Person.

P: For, somewhat as the rational soul and the body compose one man, so Christ is one Person who is both God and man;

All: Who suffered for our salvation, who descended into hell, who rose again the third day from the dead;

P: Who ascended into heaven, and sits at the right hand of God the Father almighty, from there He shall come to judge both the living and the dead.

All: At His coming all men shall rise again in their bodies, and shall give an account of their works.

P: And those who have done good shall enter into everlasting life, but those who have done evil into everlasting fire.

All: All this is Catholic faith, and unless one believes it truly and firmly one cannot be saved.

P: Glory be to the Father

All: As it was in the beginning.

Here follows a large number of psalms which may be used by the exorcist at his discretion but these are not a necessary part of the rite. Some of them occur in other parts of the Ritual and are so indicated; the others may be taken from the Psalter. Psalm 90; psalm 67; psalm 69; psalm 53; psalm 117; psalm 34; psalm 30; psalm 21; psalm 3; psalm 10; psalm 12.

Prayer Following Deliverance

P: Almighty God, we beg you to keep the evil spirit

from further molesting this servant of yours, and to
keep him far away, never to return. At your
command, 0 Lord, may the goodness and peace
of our Lord Jesus Christ, our Redeemer, take
possession of this man (woman). May we no longer
fear any evil since the Lord is with us; who lives
and reigns with you, in the unity of the Holy Spirit,
God, forever and ever.

All: Amen.

9. Deliverance

Deliverance is a form of Exorcism that is performed by many Protestant Christians. They do not believe that only ordained clergy can perform exorcisms. They believe that Jesus gave everyone the power to cast out demons. Deliverance not only focuses on possession but it also used against afflictions and negative behaviors caused by a demonic spirit's coercion and influence on a person.

<u>Prayer for Deliverance</u>

Father in the name of the Lord Jesus Christ I bring this soul before you and ask you to totally deliver

them and set them free from every demonic attack
and from every demon that has come against them.
Deliver and heal them, physically, emotionally,
financially, bodily, and spiritually.

Now I loose the Holy Spirit into every vacant place
within them. Father cover them in the blood of
Jesus and seal them until the day of redemption.

In Jesus Name, Amen!

Christian Prayer for Deliverance From Spirit Possession

Dear Heavenly Father, we acknowledge Your
presence in this room and in our lives. You are
everywhere, You are all-powerful and You know all
things. We need You, and we know that we can do
nothing without You. We believe the Bible
because it tells us what is really true. We refuse to
believe the lies of Satan. We ask you to rebuke
Satan and place a hedge of protection around this
room so we can do Your will. As children of God
we take authority over Satan and command Satan
to release (name of person) in order that (name)
can know and choose to do the will of God. In the

name of Jesus, we command Satan and all His forces to be bound and silenced within (name) so they cannot inflict any pain or in any way prevent God's will from being accomplished in (name) life. We ask the Holy Spirit to fill us and direct us into all truth. In Jesus's name we pray. Amen.

Willful Sin

Father, I ask that you cover me with the blood of JESUS and I call upon your mighty angels for protection and enforcement of your will for me, IN JESUS' NAME! Father, it is written and I believe that you are faithful to forgive me of my sins. I confess that I have willfully sinned against you since my childhood until now. Lord, I confess and renounce my willful sins of: sexual immorality, anger, pride, stubbornness, bitterness, rejection, hate, shame, contention, self-will, selfishness, division, and worldly ambition. I confess and renounce Father, that I have placed other things and people before you. Father, I worship no other god but you! Father, I ask you to forgive me of all my sin. Wash me with your blood, cleansing me of all unrighteousness. I desire to follow ONLY you Lord Jesus and to become holy. For it is written that you raise a holy nation unto yourself and be holy for you are holy. I thank you Lord for forgiving me, for washing me white as snow; for justifying and sanctifying me so that I may do your will. Father, I take authority over all unclean and foul spirits that hold themselves against you, IN THE NAME OF JESUS! I command that they leave me quietly and completely in the NAME OF JESUS. I proclaim that I belong to you Lord JESUS! I bind and cast out all demons IN THE NAME OF JESUS! Loose me, leave me, be gone IN THE NAME OF JESUS. I am forgiven; I am the redeemed of God! Thank you Father, IN THE NAME OF JESUS, Amen.

Freedom from Generational Curses

Father God, I thank you for setting the foundations of the earth; for giving life, and for giving your Son, JESUS. I belong to you Lord Jesus! I cover myself right now with your blood and call upon your mighty angels for protection and assistance. For it is written an angel of the Lord encamps around those who reverence thy name and delivers them. Thank you Lord for your angels and mercy. Father God, you said that you would visit your wrath unto the third and fourth generation from my father and my fathers father. Lord, your judgments are just and righteous. Lord God, I know that Jesus died once for all. So, I come before you asking mercy and forgiveness for the sins of:(say each known sin) and for the unknown sins and curses of my families generations. We have been a rebellious family. we have served of gods. Our sins of bitterness, anger, hatred, raged and unforgiveness have separated us from you and brought calamity to our generation. We are guilty of sexual sins. We have not treated others as we should. We have been full of self-pity, rejection, and gossip. We have stolen, lied, cheated, our iniquities have piled up beyond our measure. I confess and ask you Lord, to forgive my family line and myself. I thank you for your mercy and forgiveness. I renounce any and all generational sins and curses on myself and on the family that you gave me. I place them under the precious blood of Jesus! And ask you Lord for a new generational inheritance of health, freedom, and all spiritual blessings in Christ Jesus for myself, my family, and the generations that follow us. You are worthy Lord God of honor, praise, and glory; for you have dominion over all things. So, IN THE NAME OF JESUS and with your authority I break all generational sins and curses. In the NAME OF JESUS I command all evil spirits to loose me and my family! Leave me and my family (say each family members name) now gently and completely, In THE NAME OF JESUS! In THE NAME OF JESUS, I bind you foul spirits and cast you out! Be gone from me and my family (say each family members name) right now, IN THE NAME OF JESUS! In the NAME ABOVE EVERY NAME, JESUS, I confess, accept and believe in faith that I and my family are loosed and have a new generational inheritance of health, freedom, and all Spiritual blessings in Christ JESUS! I thank you, my Lord and my personal savior! I ask right now that the Holy Spirit fill any and all parts of my Body where any demon has left or moved, IN JESUS NAME I pray, AMEN.

Prayer For Deliverance

Heavenly Father, praise your name, Heaven and Earth bows before You. There is no name higher, my Lord and Father. I believe in You and Your Son, Jesus Christ. I believe that Jesus came into the world, a virgin birth, all righteous and holy, as our redeemer and savior. Jesus died on the cross and rose from the dead three days later, so we could be forgiven of our sins and have everlasting life in Heaven. He shed His precious blood so we could live forever and not perish as the wages of sin demand. I know that Jesus is the only way to You, God Almighty, all knowing, all caring, all loving. I renounce living my life by only my decisions.

I invite You to control my life, I willingly give up my life to Your loving hands, to use me for Your glory and honor. I know that Your unlimited forgiveness and mercy will save me from myself.

Forgive me of my sins, known and unknown, especially the sin of _____, that I will not offend You Lord. Thank You for Your mercy and forgiveness. I turn away from these sins and ask the Holy Spirit to convict me of any other sins that I am unaware of and make me know them, so I will not repeat them.

As, You have forgiven me of my sins, I forgive anyone who has wronged me. I freely give my forgiveness as forgiveness is freely given to me by You, my God of mercy. I carry no bitterness, resentment, hatred, or a desire for revenge. Bless them Lord because I know they are people like myself with weaknesses and You forgave me. I especially forgive _____ .

Jesus, my Redeemer, You spilled Your Blood that I may be saved and that I am not subject to the curses or judgements of evil intent. By Your Blood, I ask You Jesus to cancel and release me from any and all curses and judgements that bind my life from past or present causes. If I am under a curse from our Holy Father, please let it be known to me so I may repent and be forgiven. Please open the door to our Fathers' Blessings. Thank You Jesus for freeing me to receive the deliverance I need.

Armor of God

In the Name of Jesus, I break all ties with the occult and close all doors to this evil domain. By the power and authority given to me by God through his son Jesus, I declare I am bound no more by any occult sin or practice. Thank You Lord for the power and authority. I will destroy any occult or associated objects or idols in my possession.

Forgive me of any false religion or worship, known or unknown to me, that I have been involved with. Forgive me of anything that I have put above You or ahead of You. I know this is a form of bondage that I am asking to be freed from. I renounce anything in my life that has kept me from You, My God. I especially renounce _____.

I stand firm with You, my Lord. I praise Your Name and sing of Your greatness. I put on Your armor, that I may be ready to fight evil in Your Name. I submit to you my Lord, my God Almighty. Thank You Jesus for the ultimate sacrifice that You made for me. By Your act You made all things possible through our Father.

I now speak and call out any spirits or demons that are trying to control me. Any influence of evil, spirit of _____ or demon of _____, I bind you, in the Name of Jesus, Who shed His Blood to

give me the Authority to cast you out in His Name
Jesus Christ, I command you to leave now and to
go to Jesus for Him to do with you as He desires.

In the Name of Jesus I pray and give thanks for my
deliverance. AMEN

Prayer For Deliverance

Kyrie eleison. God, our Lord, King of ages, All-
powerful and All-mighty, you who made everything
and who transform everything simply by your will.
You who in Babylon changed into dew the flames
of the "seven-times hotter" furnace and protected
and saved the three holy children. You are the
doctor and the physician of our soul. You are the
salvation of those who turn to you. We beseech
you to make powerless, banish, and drive out every
diabolic power, presence and machination; every
evil influence, malefice, or evil eye and all evil
actions aimed against your servant. . . where there
is envy and malice, give us an abundance of
goodness, endurance, victory, and charity. O Lord,
you who love man, we beg you to reach out your
powerful hands and your most high and might
arms and come to our aid. Help us, who are made

in your image, send the angel of peace over us, to protect us body and soul. May he keep at bay and vanquish every evil power, every poison or malice invoked against us by corrupt and envious people. Then, under the protection of your authority may we sing, in gratitude, "The Lord is my salvation; whom should I fear?" I will not fear evil because you are with me, my God, my strength, my powerful Lord, Lord of peace, Father of all ages. Yes, Lord our God, be merciful to us, your image, and save your servant . . . from every threat or harm from the evil one, and protect him by raising him above all evil. We ask you this through the intercession of our Most Blessed, Glorious Lady, Mary ever Virgin, Mother of God, of the most splendid archangels and all yours saints. Amen."

Our Father, who art in heaven;
hallowed be Thy name;
Thy kingdom come; Thy will be
done on earth as it is in heaven.
Give us this day our daily bread;
and forgive us our trespasses as
we forgive those who trespass
against us, and lead us not into
temptation; but deliver us from
evil. Amen.

Armor of God

Armor of God